SMALL-TOWN GAY

SMALL-TOWN GAY:
essays on Family life beyond the big city

edited by
Elizabeth Newman

Kerlak Publishing
Memphis, Tennessee

SMALL-TOWN GAY: essays on Family life beyond the big city

A Kerlak Publications Book
Published by Kerlak Enterprises, Inc.
Memphis, TN

www.kerlak.com

ISBN: 0-9660744-9-1

Library of Congress Control Number: 2004112736

First Edition: August 2004

Printed in the United States of America

Copyright Acknowledgements

This book is respectfully dedicated to Brad, my brother by choice, loving friend, and the inspiration for Small-Town Gay.

Contents

Foreword

Curt Johnson

Growing up in a very small farming town, I searched desperately for a book like this in order to not feel so alone. In the 1980s, the only two books that I was able to find that defined gay culture were Larry Kramer's *Faggots* and Andrew Holleran's *Dancer From the Dance.* I knew there had to be other books out there, but these were the only two I could find, and they scared the hell out of me. They scared me since I felt that this was my future, but I kept thinking that there had to be other young men and women out there like myself who couldn't relate to the characters in those books.

I grew up on a working farm, was the quarterback on the high school football team, captain of the wrestling team, and had a really good high school experience. I knew I was gay and different from all my friends, but when I read about the characters in those books, I felt even more different from them. I was terrified that I would never fit in anywhere, or worse, that I was the only person in the world like this.

In the books I'd read, everyone was in the closet and terrified of telling anyone about themselves, fearing they would be ostracized or caused bodily harm. Of course, this is not always the case, but I've never quite followed the norm, and having to pretend to be something I was not for four more years just didn't appeal to me. It seemed easier to just be up front with it rather than have people suspect and play the taunting game that happens so often. Once you tell someone right off the bat, what can they really do? Growing up a Southern redneck, I figured I could just kick their ass if they tried something—not always the easiest or best solution, but we all have to do what works for us. And when you're young, you get away with that kind of thinking, too.

It wasn't until freshman year in college that I came out while rushing my fraternity, and surprisingly, no one batted an eye. No one was more shocked than I was when I blurted this out to my fraternity brothers and football team. I figured that if they had a problem with me based solely on that little thing, it was their problem. All I ever heard from everyone was, "*You don't seem gay to me.*" I never paid much attention to that until I started hearing it from the gay community.

When the editor of this anthology contacted me, my first comment was, "I don't know if I'm gay enough for your book." She couldn't figure out what I meant until I explained that several journalists who had written about me in the mainstream press after a documentary I produced won the 2002 Academy Award, wanted to do profiles on me for the gay press— but both *Out* magazine and *The Advocate* had informed them that I wasn't "gay enough" for them. That comment stunned me, and it made me realize that there is a great need for this type of book that shows stories outside of New York and Los Angeles, so young gay men and women realize that you don't have to be this way or that way to be gay. You just have to be yourself.

The gay community prides itself on its individualism, but when the community starts dictating what is or isn't gay, that is disturbing to me. It's confusing enough to grow up in rural America knowing you're different, but then finding out that you are further criticized if you don't adhere to certain traits within the gay community only makes things more confusing. I truly felt that I had to do the gym, dress the part, etc., to be part of the gay community, but it only made me feel more of an outsider even though I looked like everyone else. Then I realized *that* was the problem: I had lost my individuality.

After reading the powerful stories in this anthology, it makes me hope that there will be more of these books to help dispel the thinking that if you're gay, you must do this or do that to feel part of the community. I now feel more a part of the community doing things the way that I like. I still get called a "bad fag," etc., by other gay men since I still love football, mountain biking and things like that. And not every movie I produce or write will have a gay theme, but that doesn't make me or anyone else less gay than someone who is out on the front lines waving his or her rainbow flag.

We're free to make our own choices about how we live our lives without fearing that our own community will condemn us for not fitting in better. We're also free to try to fit in to that community if we choose. It's your own personal choices and opinions that determine who you are. As this book shows, being a gay man or woman is just part of who you are; it's up to each of us to determine what makes up the rest.

Editor's Note

Elizabeth Newman

The seed for this book was sown with a single question I posed to my friend over a decade ago when, at age 28, he said out loud for the very first time in his life, "I'm gay."

"But how did you ever survive?" was my response.

My friend was the All-American, blond giant—the beloved hometown basketball and tennis champion who was kind to everyone he encountered, but still managed to be cool. He was student body president and the prom king. He was the ultimate Southern small-town boy who was now in the big city, completing a graduate degree in social work to accompany his business degree, so that he could plan and direct nursing home care.

However, I have not told you the full story; my question was not my first reaction to my friend's revelation. My friend had a reputation for outrageous teasing. I recall one time when he strode purposely up to me in our graduate school lounge, and whispered, "I have something important to tell you." I had never seen him with such serious countenance, and as I braced myself for bad news, he leaned in close to my ear.

"You is crazy!" He screamed and did an exaggerated hip-hop dance. As usual, the tension that had been in the room—we were studying for our comprehensive exams at the time—dissipated, and some of the students who truly could hip-hop, turned on the radio and got up to join him. In fact, we all joined him, clapping and feeling the joy that he could so often bring into any situation.

So, on that cold Memphis night, when he leaned in close, his arm around me as he walked me to my car, and he whispered, "I have to tell you something," I was not falling for it. I must preface that just prior to this moment, he and I had attended one of the first screenings of Tom Hanks' *Philadelphia* because we were completing a project for our "Oppression" class, and by strange kismet, when the hat containing project topic slips was passed to us, our group had drawn "Discrimination Toward Lesbians and Gays" as our issue to present to the class. And, as usual, with his typical irreverence and anything but politically correct manner, my friend read out our topic with an effeminate lisp and affected a stroll, placing his arms akimbo.

So, on that cold night, when he revealed his long-held secret to me, I began playfully punching him and choking on cold air and laughter. But then I looked up at his face, and for the first time ever, I saw tears in his eyes.

I can still feel the horrible shame and panic I felt when I realized that my friend had just spoken the truth for the first time in his life, and here I was, laughing.

I hugged him close, and we went back inside. He told me that I was the only one in the world he had ever told and he did not intend for anyone else ever to know. He had been raised in a very conservative Christian church, in a very small, rural Southern town. He admitted that during his childhood, the only people whom he suspected were gay in his hometown had been a florist, a hairdresser, and a funeral director, and that he could in no way relate to the flamboyant ways in which they lived. Through an athletic scholarship, he attended a very small, fundamentalist Christian college, so he had been even farther back in the closet there. His plan had been to remain celibate and silent, but he just could not do that anymore.

"But how did you ever survive?" I asked him.

He began to tell me about how he had masked his desires by trying to excel in everything he did. He had to be the best friend, athlete, son, grandson, and employee. He hoped that by doing the best he could and by working hard to help everyone he met that he might stand a chance of still being accepted if his secret were ever discovered.

"I thought that I was the only one like me," he said about his childhood.

I was the only one who knew his secret for about a year; then, gradually, as he began to meet friends I had known from undergraduate college who were professionals and gay, he began to tell others.

Recently, he and I were discussing how far he has come: He is currently nationally ranked in the Gay Lesbian Tennis Alliance and has many friends from all over the world. He is an active fund-raiser for children and adults who have AIDS, and, of course, he is still the big, gangly man whom his friends and family always loved.

Many times over the past decade, he and I have discussed how his being raised in a small town gave him many of the qualities people love about him, but he had always known that it was most certainly a given that he would have to leave his small town in order to have a relationship openly and find community.

Just a few years ago, I began to see gay couples I knew from my days of teaching in New England start leaving the big cities and settling in smaller towns to begin raising families. I was amazed at their courage and resolve; they would be pioneers. They would most certainly meet opposition, I thought, in isolated suburban or rural life.

My friend and I started to wonder how other people who were gay and were either raised in small towns or were now living in them were coping. I put out a call for manuscripts, and just as the first essays were reaching our post box, what seemed to be a miracle appeared via CNN. Gay couples were racing to San Francisco and Massachusetts and were being allowed to marry!

I watched these couples on TV—pairs of men or women, some holding children to whom they had given birth or had adopted—racing across the country to these larger, more progressive cities, so hopeful, eager to make the commitment that heterosexual couples often take for granted. I wondered how many of them would have to return to hometowns that would never accept or acknowledge the marriage or civil union licenses they now possessed. I wondered…

Then, last month, I saw a proposed amendment to the Constitution that would have restricted the term "marriage" to mean exclusively a union between a man and a woman fail because so many people, gay and straight, objected and voiced their objections to their representatives.

The contributors to this anthology have stood up in different ways—some on the front lines; some simply by surviving and living to tell about it now. I am grateful to them for sharing their stories. I admire them all for their courage to share their truths. My hope is that their stories will reach others who need to hear them.

I am a therapist who practices in a small, rural community in the South. One of the problems that troubles me most these days is the high rate of suicide and suicide attempts among teenagers and young adults. Those of us in the field know that a significant number of these adolescents and young adults attempt to end their lives because they are struggling with defining and/or accepting their sexuality.

This book is by no means a substitute for real talk or counseling by responsible, professionally-trained and caring adults, but I do hope that these stories reach anyone who feels as isolated as my friend did, and who is challenged by the questions: *Can I be what I am and be accepted*? *Can I keep trying for another day, another month, another year, until I can find a place or a supportive community where I can feel comfortable*? *Can I be patient enough with myself to understand that sexuality is not always clearly defined—and could evolve throughout my lifetime—and that I might have to struggle before I create a life that is the ideal for me*? And, most importantly, *Will I value my life enough not to end it even though I don't completely know or understand the answers right now*?

On a lighter note, I hope that those readers who have themselves journeyed through the joys and perils of small-town living will enjoy and relate to these stories, and they will share them with others.

Lastly, I am pleased and honored to have been (sometimes) the first reader of some of these talented authors' manuscripts. I thank Kerlak Publishing for giving these authors a chance to share their stories.

The authors made this book. I only asked the question.

Elizabeth Newman,
Memphis, Tennessee, 3 August 2004

Start With a Farm

Darin Beasley

And see snow across the fields and beyond the barn all the way into the woods. The morning is awake with snow coming down. The snow falls around your grandmother's front porch where you stand with her. Her name is Margaret. She wears her red cardigan and a heavy winter coat. The two of you have had toast and eggs and she has given you a small cup of Sanka. (She lets you put the decaffeinated grinds into the teacups, and you get to stir the hot water, too.) You sat in the chair beside her where you can look out the window, and now she is getting you bundled up for your walk home.

It doesn't snow in South Carolina very often, so you're never prepared. There are galoshes, but none fit your small feet. Margaret has saved plastic Sunbeam Bread bags for years. On each of your feet she puts one bag after another until they make a thick layer. Once each Sunbeam snowshoe is finished, she takes large rubber bands and twists them around your ankles, folding the top plastic over and tucking that under the rubber bands. She gives you a kiss and sends you on your way. You are walking to your parents' house which is also on the farm, but that house is not as old as your grandmother's one-story.

There is no house like the farmhouse.

There is no one like Margaret, and you are in love with her.

Whenever you look over your shoulder, you see her standing on the porch where you parted company. Margaret has the bluest eyes you have ever seen. She is watching to be certain you make it home safely in the cold by yourself. You wave to each other. You want to turn around and go back to her.

The farm is one of many farms that make up a rural community called Stokes Bridge. Depending on the season, fields of cotton, tobacco, soybeans or wheat separate the farms, their houses, and families.

Stokes Bridge does not have a bridge.

Some of the roads in Stokes Bridge are paved but none of them have names.

Pecan trees make a magnificent impression when you look up towards the sky, the same sky that runs above the entire earth, above every place, including the two towns you call your hometowns. Because of the farm's location, your family's phone number belongs to one town and your address says you reside in the other. One town, the smaller of the two, is called Bishopville. This is where you go to a private school that looks like a prison. This is where your mother likes to shop and you get new clothes at a department store called Belk's when every school year starts. The larger town is called Hartsville. It sits in the heart of Darlington County. Your birth certificate says you were born there. Hartsville's got a little more going for it than Bishopville. There's better shopping and a college is there too. Margaret went to the college for one year in the 1920s but left because the gym teacher made the girls' gym class strip in an inappropriate manner. Margaret was appalled and chose a better place to finish her studies. Still, the college exerts a pull on your family. Your mother will soon attend the college part-time and train in soprano (she sounds like a classical bird when she sings). You do not know this now, but you, your brother and sister will all graduate from this college (there you will meet freaks from all over the country who poke fun at the heavy twang in your voice, you will fall in love with your best friend, a straight guy who's a drama major and drives a convertible.) You are so young right now you will not know a lot of things for a long time. They all will come one by one.

One fact is obvious though. South Carolina is fascinating and repulsive. One direction gives you a magnolia blossom in a vase on a lady's kitchen table and the other direction sends out a squirt of tobacco juice from a farmer's mouth. When you go to Bishopville and Hartsville you leave the magnolia and the tobacco juice worlds behind (some people don't, but that's because the South is composed of two types of people: those with manners and those without). Were you not to behave at your very best in either town, your bottom will find you crying once you get back home. That's a story your bottom has told many times over. You are five.

And going on six years old.

At your chickadee age, everything fits together nicely until one day *The Wonderful World of Disney* works its not-so-innocent magic. It is a Sunday night and supper is finished. The Disney movie introduces you to a very good-looking Kurt Russell (you want to be his character, Dexter with the invisible potion), fun beach parties and palm trees—palm trees that are nothing like the palmetto trees in South Carolina. In the West, the palm trees are taller than buildings and they practically kiss the sky.

After that momentous viewing, whenever the television is on, you keep your ears tuned for any mention of California. You are mesmerized by the idea of Hollywood. You teach yourself how to tap dance and tell your mother that you will never learn to drive a car because you are going to live in California and have a chauffeur. She says "Ha," and takes the biscuits out of the oven. She has no idea, but you've already wrapped your mind, body, and soul into California. In the meantime, you reconfigure your practical nature with your dreamier longings. Whatever you look at in South Carolina you adorn with a California nametag. You will talk to Margaret about California whenever the opportunity presents itself. Although you lack the words that describe the feelings you experience being under her gaze, you understand something about Margaret—she believes in following your heart even if it belongs somewhere else. She says, "Tell me about California."

Meanwhile, the two of you watch winter turn to summer. When you are both tanned and the sun lingers way into the evening hours, you sit on her front porch and shell peas from the garden.

But you know it will never be the same. You have tasted something fresh, golden and far enough out of reach to make you desire it more than anything you have ever wished for.

During the summer, you are on the farm more often than not. The two towns you're sandwiched between are for special errands—so you go one way or the other two or three times a week. That leaves four full days of Stokes Bridge. It's home to good company, talking about things you cannot comprehend. Your company includes, but is not limited to, sun-burnt farmers and church-going ladies who, if they are your mother's age and sassy, smoke cigarettes when the men aren't looking. This microcosm isn't the most exciting place, but it has its fair share of adventure.

Your exotic aunt who's Hispanic flies out from Texas to visit. She has fancy dresses and loves how you never want to stop talking with her. But one night you make a mistake. Around dinner time, she comes out of the bedroom wearing a wig and you laugh at her. She runs through the hallway in the opposite direction, crying.

You have laughed at someone you idolize, someone who respects you. You feel you can't do enough to make it up to her. Every morning you make the guest bed, at mealtimes you pull out her chair for her, and in the early hot afternoons, you pour her a glass of sweet iced tea and wedge a lemon slice on the side of the glass, the way she likes it. The sun sets anyway.

Your aunt is only here for a week and a half. Every night the same guy wearing a nice shirt and tie picks her up in his car with the top down. They have lots of dates. They drive away to Hartsville or maybe even Florence, a bigger city you can never call your town because it is too far away. Florence means serious shopping days (lawn mowers, wedding china) or important doctor visits (broken arms, major stitches).

Bishopville is where your family doctor's office is located.

Bishopville is not a mysterious town.

Hartsville, on the other hand, has a history and a present you find much more fascinating. Hartsville is where Margaret taught first grade for thirty-three years, an accomplishment that amazes you. There are restaurants in the town. And you have gone to the cinema many times. Your first adult film is *Airport.* The cinema on Main Street is your widescreen dream.

You fall in love with Hartsville because everything there feels like the town has raised its hand and volunteered to be your tiny version of California. In a moment of candor, you are pleased to discover that Margaret prefers Hartsville to Bishopville as well.

Hartsville is bigger than you. Other places and things that are bigger than you will reveal themselves one day. You just have to hold tight.

When you go to Hartsville, Margaret drives the car.

Margaret likes to go on Saturdays, and there is not a Saturday you are not with her. You park outside the Winn-Dixie and enter through the electric doors. Margaret looks at her grocery list. You help her get items from the shelves and put them into the cart. She gives you a LifeSaver. After the groceries are stored away in the car trunk comes the best moment of all. You now have three-quarters of an hour to find something you want, anything you want that's priced within reason, in the best store on the planet: Roses.

Roses, no other joy can compare.

The store's name is in blue letters and there's a big blue swirl around that.

Roses makes you think of California because it has toys you see advertised on the television. Toys, board games, records and paper dolls.

Dolls, dolls, dolls: one side of you is a sissy.

Just as big is the side of you that likes toy tractors and B.B. guns and footballs.

Somehow you are going to be more than just a little man. You are not going to give anything up, at least not yet. After all, your family knows and they do not care, they say it's a phase and your father had baby dolls when he was a wee one during the Great Depression.

It's other people who think it's odd. You are becoming familiar with the art of the raised eyebrow. You've seen men, women and children all raise an eyebrow when the subject turns to paper dolls. Is it shame or confusion or both you feel? You can't say. You believe in California and run to Margaret.

There is nowhere to run in Bishopville or Hartsville.

Myrtle Beach, however, offers a truer sense of running. Here, you run wild, kicking sand and splashing through the shallow waves that break on the shore.

People come from all over the East Coast to do the same thing.

Like anyone entranced by the sun and craving cold water, each summer your family packs up and heads for the beach. Myrtle Beach. The waves seem gigantic. You can't swim so you don't go out far. Your father takes you out and holds your hand and so does your brother. Your mother is sunbathing, your sister is showing off swimming, and Margaret is sitting partway under a striped umbrella. She has surprised you. She wears a black one-piece bathing suit and you love how she looks like a woman and not necessarily your grandmother. Your crush deepens when you realize there is more to her than you know. She is in her sixties and out here with the summer girls like it's easy. She has suntan lotion and tells you it's called Coppertone.

Later on in the day something strange happens.

You are covered in sand and you follow your father and brother into a men's changing room. After all that sun outside it feels dark and cool. Lights hang from the ceiling and showers wet the floor. Your father is goofy and not bashful getting undressed. Other men, most of them your father's age, are taking off their bathing suits, standing under the showerheads or drying themselves off with beach towels. You have never seen so many naked men in your life. Not only are you surrounded by naked men, they're comfortable—so comfortable it seems like there are thousands of men around you, thousands of men you somehow know, men who have the same apparatus as you. The feeling has exploded inside in your chest like a bomb. You take off your swimming trunks and have to look down at what you've got. You are dizzy.

Breaking through this spell is your father's voice. He tells you to hurry up, the women will be waiting. What is regular about your life has returned and you are okay with that. You reach into the canvas tote for your clothes.

That night you hear the sound of waves through the open windows. You are watching television in a bedroom you and Margaret share in the two-story house your family has rented. The television show concerns a bachelor father family. Everyone in the cast looks happy and wears nice clothes.

Some of the people you see on the beach look like the actors on the bachelor father show. The people are not without flaws, but they are attractive. The world is alluring and calling to you and it's not just what you see, either. You hear strange sounding accents when you walk on the boardwalk. You want to ask everyone where they come from.

Bishopville and Hartsville have a long way to go, but you know where you come from. The farm is different. The farm belongs to your family. No one else but your family can take or add anything to the farm.

It is the middle of the night. You wake up and your stomach is growling. Margaret asks you where you are going at this hour. You say you want a glass of milk, and she lets you find your way by yourself. Your feet are bare and feel free on the carpeted stairs. You are wide awake in the dark house. If you wanted, you could slip out and make a run for the ocean.

In the fall, when you return to school in Bishopville, there's still something un-nameable about yourself and men, but you are too young to get it or care. Your childhood obsessions, like playing and studying hard, distract you and pull you back into the world where you belong, where there are other more important things to comprehend, math and spelling and something about history, perhaps Christopher Columbus. You have heard of him, but you are getting good at pretending these days. You will learn to pretend a lot in Bishopville.

For now, though, you live for normal days, snacking on peanut-butter sandwiches and learning how to spell, getting new paper dolls and throwing the soft, old football with your sister. You watch all the fruit trees in Margaret's yard blossom. You teach yourself how to ride a bike. You are a regular kind of little man—with a light burning inside now.

You let the burn go down to a flame and hold it inside so that it does not go out.

Until the next strange day appears, there is school all week, there is Hartsville on the weekends, and the farm in between. A little sow, Isabelle, is your co-star when Margaret is busy with something and needs you to take care of yourself.

The farm is a perpetual in-between and it fits snug this way. The farm holds all of you together, and mostly you and Margaret in the house she has lived in for what feels like the longest time. One room in her house has a champagne-colored carpet. You want to make time last. You pray for Margaret and California to last forever.

Shikse Tomboy

Hawk Madrone

We had music class just once each week in the third grade at Walnut Street Elementary. The boys at the bigger desks in the back of the room got to help Miss Weikert carry out the songbooks from the cabinet; Mr. Clark, the stern school principal we feared most of the time, came to our room to play the piano. It was the only time we were ever encouraged to be loud, so we belted out "Old McDonald Had a Farm" with stored-up gusto and created a gleeful cacophony with "Row, Row, Row Your Boat," sung as a three-part round. Hard for me to learn was the song about the Hatfields and McCoys. Both the words and the tune refused to slide into my memory as easily as the oink-oinks of McDonald's pigs, and the simple repetitions of "row" and "merrily." I did not really understand what the song was about, except that these two Sleepy Hollow families had some problem between them, and I figured it would have been tough to be a kid attached to both.

I was not a Hatfield or a McCoy, and Hanover—population 16,000 or so, located in the central southern farm country of Pennsylvania—was a step up from a sleepy hollow. But I knew something about living on the cusp where disparate families overlapped.

My mother was a Shanabrook, my father a Blumenthal. Mom came from a long line of Western European Lutheran Gentiles; Daddy was the second eldest son of Russian Jewish immigrants. One condition Mom had made when they married in 1934 was that their children would be raised Lutheran, so my older brother was spared circumcision, and I was singing "Jesus loves me, this I know, for the Bible tells me so" almost as soon as I could talk. Some of the Jewish Blumenthals were substantially better off than most of the Lutheran Shanabrooks; by the time I was old enough to visit cousins on my own, I painfully learned that I was somewhat more an outsider to the Blumenthals, who called me a *mishugeneh shikse* than I was even to the Shanabrooks, whose working class sense of aspirant lady-likeness just barely tolerated my whistling tomboy swagger. The other people of the town who knew me saw me as the daughter of a Jew, and therefore a Jew, the ones who killed Christ, the ones all that uproar was being made about in Germany, sending some of their sons home in coffins. "Crazy gentile," a "Christ-killer"—my confused sense of whom I belonged to, who my people were, made even treasured summer mornings at the neighborhood playground into possibilities for wrenching choices. Sometimes I laughed with the other kids when they told a "Jew joke;" sometimes I went home horrified, crying.

"What are you brutzin' about now?" Mom asked one of those times, impatient with her housework.

"One of the boys said some awful things about Jews, that they are stingy and they aren't real Americans, and..." then sniffing hard, "Mom, am I a Jew?" wiping my nose on my sleeve.

"How many times have I told you not to use your clothes for a hanky?" Then, softening a little, "And, no, you have to have a Jewish mother to be a Jew."

"But Daddy's a Jew, and Bubbi and Zaidie," I said referring to the names I knew my grandparents by.

"And that's nothing to cry about. Your Daddy's people are good people. Why, do you know when they came over here they had nothing but what they could carry, and Zaidie started out collecting scrap door-to-door?"

"What'd he do that for?"

"So he could sell it, of course. He saved his money, kept at it, and worked his way up to opening the clothing store. He didn't let somebody else's attitude send him home crying."

The next Jew joke I heard, I neither laughed nor cried, but stored away some bitter knowledge that being different could be costly.

Except for an occasional special dinner or barbecue with my father's people, it was the Shanabrooks who dominated the family events of my Pennsylvania years. In the autumn, Mom's two sisters and two brothers and all their families got together at Caledonia State Park for a big picnic, ball games, hikes in the woods, and nearly endless laughter. The Thanksgiving, Christmas, and Easter feasts my mother rose early to prepare, fed aunts, uncles, cousins, and her father, Papaw, who was widowed when I was an infant. Some country farmers, but most living in town, mother's people were hard-working people, the men sweating in shoe factories or spinning mills, or trying to make a go of it with a corner luncheonette. The women tended their houses and broods, with brief summer jobs in the canning factories, and grew what they could in their small backyard gardens. They believed that nothing came for free, that disappointment was needed to balance pride.

By eleven, I joined this workforce by being assigned housecleaning chores that had to meet my mother's hard-won approval. Though I loved fixing the upright vacuum cleaner when its belt periodically slipped from the pulley, I was bored with dusting the furniture, dawdled over the blue-glass-topped coffee table. My reflection became a Saturday morning inspiration for fantasizing myself in a life where I could be who I wanted to be. I imagined my urge to perform daredevil feats on my fat-tire bicycle met with parental applause instead of worry disguised as disapproval; dreamed the Shaeffer girls would not laughingly reject me at the Saturday night dances long after I was supposed to have outgrown the desire for girl-partners; saw myself decked out in button-down shirts and khaki trousers, my hands gallant and comfortable in the pockets made deep enough for the odds and ends necessary for field, street, and alley games.

My reveries were most often interrupted by my overworked mother, so I would refocus on the tedious labor to earn my weekly allowance of a quarter, twelve cents of which bought me a double-dip ice cream cone at the small neighborhood grocery store.

In the landscape of my childhood, there were alleyways and outhouses, roses and peonies, bush beans and scallions, a white spirea hedge between our house and the shoe factory on euphemistically named Terrace Avenue. We did not own an automobile until I was a senior in high school, so, until a birthday brought that Z-tire bike, walking was a given: walking with my mother no matter the weather to St. Paul's Evangelical on Sunday mornings and to choir practice there mid-week evenings; walking uptown to the Strand Theater for the Saturday afternoon cowboy movies; walking to grade school and junior high across town, then to high school even farther. It must have been a Saturday when I, still a pre-teen, was walking on my way to the movie theater: down Terrace a block and a half to Baer and past the playground, then another two blocks up Baer to Broadway, eventually on up to the Square and uptown Hanover. As I approached the intersection of Baer and Broadway, I noticed a woman come out of a house on the corner, get in a car, and drive away. I knew I was watching a woman, but her short ash-blonde hair had a barber's cut; her light brown double-breasted suit coat and trousers fit her small frame with the look of habit and familiarity. Back then, in the late 1940s, no woman I knew dressed in slacks in public, except at family picnics. Certainly no one but men wore the kind of clothes this woman wore, the kind sold in Zaidie's Hanover Men's Clothing Store, where my father and three uncles clerked. During the few short moments it took the woman to walk from the wooden door to the sedan, I scrutinized the softness of her fine-featured face, her smooth and easy step that played a subtle rhythm with the cloth of her trouser legs. I envied her combed-back hair and focused, enraptured, on her hand as her slender fingers gripped the chrome handle and pulled open the heavy door with the ease of confident muscle. She drove off.

I would never see her again, but the magnetic image of her stayed protected in my mind, until one day I risked describing her to Mom, in hopes she could tell me more about this woman, so different from all my kin. "Oh, that's Elsie," she clipped. "You stay away from her," she said, her voice a scold. I knew not to ask any further. I suspected there was a growing part of me that my mother would not embrace. I suspected that there existed outside the parameters of both the Blumenthals and Shanabrooks another world, a kind of people, and that there were possibilities and choices I would have to learn about on my own. But the learning was not so easy. Obstacles abounded at those dances at the Y, as well as in my older brother's scoffing when I yearned to play football with his buddies. I was not very welcomed by the boys when I wanted to join their marbles game at recess on the grade school playground, and I often got into trouble when asserting myself beyond other's definitions of acceptable feminine behavior.

I did have a small collection of marbles, even if my dull shooter could not compare with the polished agates of my fourth-grade competitors. Though I often went home with a few more marbles than I'd started with, the boys did not like losing to a mere girl, and I was soon teased out of the ring. As for those after-school football games, I only got as far as being allowed to play center, which meant I got to heist the ball from between my legs at the start of play, only to be immediately shoved to the ground, my face and knees hitting the grass as the teams scrambled for the ball. My mother complained about my scuffed knees and often-torn clothing, insisting football was no game for a girl. She also declared, "Girls don't whistle," when I shrilly entertained myself through chores.

Mumblypeg required a pocketknife, which I did not have, and knew better than to ask for on my Christmas wish list. But my next-door cousins, Larry and Danny, grudgingly let me use theirs one morning as they and a few other neighborhood boys gathered on a grassy patch in the shadow of the Winters' shed beside the alley, more than half-way up the block on our short street. I do not remember what was used for the target ring laid out on the ground—maybe a circle of string or a piece of rope—nor do I recall who got to begin this test of skill, a pecking order subtly established by early male bonding. I watched the boys, all close to my just-pre-teen years, take turns tossing the knife, the point of the blade sometimes soundlessly piercing the earth for a scoring point, more often landing on its side in a flat thunk and a lost turn. The challenge was to duplicate whatever special twist the lead-off player had accomplished, which could vary from a simple drop from shoulder-height to a fancy flip from the chin.

Brian Winters was the snotty kid from the nicer house at the corner of Terrace and Fulton whose shed was commandeered for this more dangerous play, not likely endorsed by any of our parents. He probably did not own a pocketknife either, and was included in the game primarily for the excuse to use the cover of the shed. Brian was no better at this sport than I was, though his reason may not have been for want of a knife to practice with, as was the case with me. Apparently he thought he should have been better, or maybe picking on the sole girl in that brood of toughies was the only way he had of feeling like he belonged. When it was his turn to try to match the flip executed flawlessly by a more skillful contender, Brian aimed the knife directly (but clumsily) at my feet instead of within the designated area. I must already have been piqued by Brian's teasing banter and the boys' reluctance to let me play, because when he purposefully threw that knife in my direction, I exploded. No matter that the knife had failed to hit me. The intent to harass was infuriating. I may have broken my mother's strict taboo and yelled, "Damn you!" as I attacked, grabbed my assailant and threw him to the ground. That scuffle ended the game, at least for Brian and me. Adrenalin carried me away from the shed, while Brian picked himself up and went crying up the concrete walk to his back door.

By afternoon I had calmed, and, grateful that my cousins had not snitched about my rough-housing, I was hanging out with them and their kid sister, Patsy, on the sidewalk in front of our house. We might have been playing catch or daring each other to imaginative perils when I noticed Brian half-walking, half being dragged alongside his father, coming down from the corner. Mr. Winters was looking right at me as he pushed his son to our concrete steps where I stood my ground as the other kids backed away. "Hit her!" the father commanded the son. I could see the fear growing in Brian's eyes, perhaps weighing the bigger threat: his father's wrath or mine. Then the man grabbed my arms and pinned them behind my back. "Go on, hit her!" he yelled. Brian just stood there, the power of my glare apparently the winning threat.

The incident dissolves then in my memory. I am sure the Winters left the scene and no one dared to hit me. I came away from that day knowing that life could come at me with the unexpected and shocking, that not fitting into the then girl-appropriate mold would put me at risk for punishment I had better learn to anticipate.

My parents, my brother, and I, and later my little sister, lived in two different houses in my growing up. The first one, on Fulton Street, was a rental, though I didn't understand that until we had to move out because the owner was selling. Suddenly, I realized that home was not guaranteed, that it could be taken away, that I could lose a whole neighborhood, a school; that in one day the movers' truck could separate me from my house on Fulton Street and Trolley-Car Hill behind our backyard, where, in the winter, I raced my sled against the boys (and often won). I remember waiting in the little living room of that first house, which was not really our house, while Mom took a phone call, a rare event, from Daddy down at the clothing store. I remember Mom's excitement and relief after the call, when she explained that Zaidie was giving to Daddy and Sam, one of his brothers, the money for the down payment on a double brick house. Uncle Sam, Aunt Barb, and my four cousins were also a Jewish-Gentile mix: Aunt Barb had been raised Methodist. Unlike my mother, Barb attached herself a little more firmly to the Blumenthals. She took on as much as she could of the Judaism that came to our small town by way of an imported rabbi on the holy days. She brought up her children as Jews, complete with Bar Mitzvahs for the boys.

Sam and Barb's family and ours shared a wall in that Terrace Avenue duplex for the next twenty years, with wooden bannisters that divided both the front and back porches, and a short wire fence that split the back yard down the middle. Most days, my mother and Aunt Barb would take a few breaks from their endless work of cleaning, laundering, cooking, baking, and sewing to sit together over a cup of coffee. One or the other of them would yell across the bannister on the back porch: "Want a cup?" which was always met by a grateful "Sure," and the awkward climb over the worn railing to the other's kitchen. Their klatches, as they called them, were a ritual that gave them a camaraderie of complaint in the drudgery of their housewiving lives, and that schooled me well when I was home and listened in.

There was always enough to eat in my mother's kitchen, though not always what I liked to eat. The reward of cakes and pies from her weekly baking required that I finish the boiled spinach at supper, and not just fill up on the creamy buttered mashed potatoes, fried chicken, or hamburg fritters. Many Saturdays, I joined with neighborhood kids in a vigorous game of "fort" in the unmowed field across the street, or I played "secret club" with Patsy, and Mitzi from around the corner. If it was raining, I sometimes watched my mother's hands, sticky with dough, roll out the shells for the sour cherry pies that were my favorite.

Our house was my mother's domain, the kitchen a fiefdom in which she ruled my reluctant ironing of my father's handkerchiefs, later graduating to his shirts and the homemade skirts and blouses I was required to wear to school. Her aluminum pots and pans bore the scratches of the metal spoons that stirred the green beans and ham hocks or beef pot pie, and of the curly brass scrubber I used when my chore was doing the supper dishes.

Sometimes on Sunday mornings after church, we walked the few additional blocks to Bubbi's kitchen, entering by the back door, never the front. We sat at her formica table while she busied herself to feed us. Sometimes it was a lunch of latkes, the potatoes grated to a pulp and fried; sometimes the thick sweetness of taigelach, each hard dough ball wrested from the cooked honey in the cold jar kept in the refrigerator. Bubbi's Yiddish accent, as thick as the honey syrup, sounded like a foreign language to me. She was also very hard of hearing, so communication between us never got much past our quick hugs hello and good-bye, and my attempt to shout a thank you loud enough for her to understand, which she only sometimes did. I wished so much for her to be a doting grandma to me, someone who would pull me onto her lap and love me just because I was her granddaughter. But though Bubbi generously shared the food in her kitchen, she never seemed particularly interested in me, and never made a welcome of her lap.

The rest of Bubbi and Zaidie's house was mostly a mystery to me. We were not invited into the bedrooms upstairs, except when Zaidie was sick and we all quietly trouped up to say hello. We rarely visited in the living room at the front of the house, kept darkened by heavy drapes so that the sun would not fade the rich satin upholstery of the furniture. Each year at Pesach, Bubbi made Passover dinner for her five children and fifteen grandchildren on two separate nights: The families with both parents being real Jews come on one night, and us in the double-house on the other.

On this special occasion, we all sat down to a meal of several courses in the large dining room, with the polished silver samovar brought from the old country in the corner and the red Mogen David wine glowing in crystal glasses. Zaidie sat at the head of the table, from where he presided over the ritual of prayer and story telling and eating. Each year, a piece of matzoh lay hidden in the cushions of his big armed chair, each year found by a grandson. I knew I was not supposed to look for it, though I was not sure if that was because I was a girl or because I was not as much a Jew as the ceremonied boys. I loved the rich and unfamiliar food: the tzimmes, grated carrots, apples, and raisins, the potato. I loved Zaidie's nasal Hebrew chanting that held ancient history in its tones, so unlike the tortured formal harmonies that came from the choir loft on those Lutheran Sunday mornings. I loved the admittance, if only for one day a year, into the secret places of my grandparents' lives.

Secret places, the places I was kept out of: the hearts of some of the bigoted townspeople, the legacy of my Semitic heritage, the inner chambers of high school cliques. When I began to chafe at the conventional assumptions and expectations of all of them, I invented secret places of my own. Sometimes I'd escape my brother's teasing about what a tomboy I was, or the admonitions from my Mom or an aunt about my future. ("Wait 'til you're married and have kids; you'll see.") I'd walk down Factory Street a couple blocks to the big tree in the cow pasture that butted up against our edge of town. I'd pull myself up into the ample branches where I could sit securely in a fork and daydream scenes of women in trousers, women in work shirts, women with muscles flexed in the sun, riding horses on the open range, going about their lives unmolested by male egos. I nurtured places inside myself where I could be neither a Shanabrook nor a Blumenthal, places that allowed me to imagine a life free of back bannisters and coffee breaks, the uneasiness of darkened living rooms, the shunning from schoolmates because of all the ways I was different, the restraints of small-town minds.

About Ben

Stacey Waite

When I was fourteen, I had a girlfriend named Chrissy. She was from Smithtown, three miles west of my own small town where I was a Z. Cavaricci-wearing, suburban junior high schooler who spent her Friday nights at the Commack Roller Rink with teased hair and hot pink skate wheels. But not with Chrissy. To Chrissy, I was Ben—Axl Rose-looking, piano-playing, poem-writing Ben with long brown hair and peach fuzz above the lip. She loved me. She loved the way I sang "Stairway to Heaven" on her answering machine and wore a bulky black leather jacket. "I want to see you with your shirt off," she says. And Chrissy doesn't know how she's on to something, how definition rests itself tightly rolled in the socks I have zipped into the crotch of my big brother's Wranglers. Chrissy says I have a gentle kiss, says her brother will kick my ass if he finds out we are "frenching."

I am afraid I had to leave her, though, one Saturday evening outside the Sports Plus Entertainment Hall. I had to leave her standing there beneath the blinking green ticket sign. She was asking too many questions, and the little bullets beneath the Ace bandage wrapped around my back and chest were ready to fire forth, and I knew it. "But we kissed," Chrissy says. I tell her I can't help it. My parents are making me move to Manhasset, which is a good thirty minutes away. I ask her for the photo her friend Emily took of me smoking at Caleb Smith Park. She must have no evidence of Ben. I tell her I don't want the photo to be painful for her. She refuses to give it over. I tell her I will call, but I can't risk it. The phone is dangerous when my father picks it up while I am talking to Chrissy. "Stacey, I need the phone," he might say. And what would happen to me then, sitting in those Z. Cavariccis with that hair and creating the life of Ben? Ben's father, after all, had died. His mother was a waitress, and his step-father hit him. Ben had it hard. Ben had only one other girlfriend before named Lisa. She was short and had braces, but Ben didn't mind. Ben was sensitive, didn't care about things like looks. Ben wrote long, beautiful poems about not-so-beautiful girls. Ben did have a cousin named Stacey. Ben tells Chrissy she might see her sometime and she will know the girl is his cousin because they look exactly alike. Ben is meticulous, covers all the bases. And when he walks away from her that Saturday, he dies a little, even at fourteen. He dies because he has lost everything.

The Lady of the House

David-Matthew Barnes

Despite my hunger, I answer the telephone in the kitchen.

"We have a very exciting offer for you. May I speak to the lady of the house?"

I clear my throat, notice a smudge on the side of the refrigerator, and answer, "There is no lady of the house."

"Oh." The woman on the other end of the phone is surprised. "We have you down as being a married couple. You're not married?"

I look over at my partner, sitting at the dinner table where he is waiting patiently for the intrusion to end. "Not legally."

She isn't happy with my answer, or she chooses to ignore it. "So, you're divorced?"

I twist the phone cord around my index finger and pull tightly. "I'm not interested in whatever it is that you're selling. My dinner is getting cold."

She sighs, defeated. "I'll put you down as single."

My back straightens. My stomach grumbles. "I'm not single."

Hope shoots through her voice. "Well, maybe your girlfriend will be interested..."

I feel my jaw tighten. "I don't have a girlfriend."

"No?"

"No. Not even in high school."

She breathes deep again, exhales her words. "I'm sorry, sir. I'm just a little confused."

Months earlier, a new life beckons to us from the safety of our politically correct California. There, we are labeled domestic partners. We have joint medical benefits. We have the right to adopt children. We are welcomed without a second glance at Christmas parties, romantic restaurants, church services. Our relationship is understood, does not require definition and is not questioned. We are two men who are in love and have made a commitment to make a life together. We are a family of our own, in the truest sense of the word.

We say good-bye to the sunny shores of California where the real estate is priced too high and our chance to live out the American dream is too low. We explore, investigate, contemplate and discuss our opportunities. We want to buy a house. We want to work at better jobs. We want to breathe in clean air. We want a sense of newness, adventure. Finally, it is decided that Georgia has been weighing heavy on our minds. We embark on a new journey to the Bible Belt, to a place where civil rights were once violently opposed. To the land of Scarlett O'Hara, the Confederate flag, the empire of peaches.

We move to a small town in Georgia, a suburb thirty miles south of Atlanta. Though the city is close, the cultures are worlds apart.

Life in a small town. Life in the South. Life in a small town in the South. At once, I find it difficult to adjust. I search for my niche, my purpose, my new identity. I revel in the quiet and simultaneously resist it. I wrap my fingers around the solitude of a simple life, while I feel the hands of the South wrap around my neck, draining every drop of the Pacific Ocean from my nostalgic veins. The monotony gives way to insomnia until my restlessness wears the carpet thin from my night-long bouts of reruns of *Roseanne* and daring dreams of big cities.

I surrender to a suburban life. My partner and I buy a house, our first. It is the permanent anchor that I hope will give me a much needed sense of home. I repeat the words like a mantra: We are living the American dream. I force my urban thoughts to become rural, numbing them down.

I notice them immediately: those fleeting moments that occur in social settings when I am forced to realize that my relationship with another man is easier to understand if it is conventionally defined.

The woman from the welcoming committee appears on our door step on a Saturday morning. As a token of friendship, she offers me a beautiful gift basket. "Make sure you give your wife the hand cream. It's from Avon. She'll love it." I explain that I don't have a wife or a girlfriend. She seems puzzled, glancing over her charted list of new residents. "Hmmm...it says here there are two adults in the house."

The waitress at the pizzeria is intrigued by us. She wants to know if we are brothers, best friends, related somehow. She does not seem satisfied with our vague replies. She ponders this from where she stands behind the cash register, watching us share a pepperoni and sausage pizza. As if we were on a date.

The cashier at the hardware store is concerned. We are buying three gallons of paint. She gently tells us, "I think it would be wise to check with your wives. They might not like these colors."

The harmless hostess at the restaurant up the road always greets us with "Just the two of you?" On our sixth visit, my partner politely informs her, "It will always be just the two of us." She responds with, "I know a lot of single women. Very nice girls."

Colorful and friendly brochures arrive in the mailbox, inviting us to attend local churches. Each one states that all families are welcome. I turn each brochure over and read in italicized words that their congregation is devoutly committed to bringing prayer back to schools, strengthening the core of traditional family values and following the word of God. Also, it is their divine hope to rid the world of sins like abortion, divorce, infidelity, violence and homosexuality.

Our homeowners association throws a holiday party, a social mixer to give us an opportunity to meet our neighbors. The festive gathering is held in one of the over-decorated model homes. My partner and I enter the party and the room is silenced with a sudden hush.

Babies are picked up. Purses are fetched. Ties are straightened. Invisible wrinkles in Christmas sweaters are smoothed out with nervous hands. He and I stand, side by side, offering genuine smiles to the room full of inquisitive strangers. It is our gregarious loan officer who finally breaks the uncomfortable silence with, "It's about time the two of you got here. I hope you're not mad that we started the party without you. Let me introduce you to everyone."

Within weeks, our inquisitive neighbors come by our yard to comment on our beautiful lawn and garden, asking my partner for landscaping tips. They stop by to borrow a ladder. They love the color we've chosen for our living room and kitchen and want to find out where we got it. They picked up one too many flats of flowers and they're sure we could use another.

We are greeted daily with warm smiles and friendly waves. We are invited to pool parties, get-togethers and any excuse for a barbecue. All Southern-style, of course.

Homosexuals. We search for them, like fellow members of a secret society. Two women shopping together in Wal-Mart arguing over spaghetti sauce and cake pans. The effeminate waiter at the local steakhouse who always brings us extra honey butter and dinner rolls. The male receptionist at the doctor's office who wears salmon-colored polo shirts with his collar turned up in defiance. The college-boy cashier at the fast food restaurant who flirts a little too much, winks a little often, and stares at my partner and me with both envy and admiration. They are our comfort, our reassurance, our silent best friends, brothers and sisters. Geography has made us a breed of our own. In another time and place, we wouldn't give each other the time of day. Here, we have an unspoken bond.

As a year passes, I am forced to accept the fact that my quality of life has improved beyond measure. I reluctantly agree that moving to the South was the best decision for us. My partner has a stellar job. I have completed and published my first novel and have already started on a second. We have our own home. The air is indeed clean and the stars shine so bright at night that it's impossible to resist the beauty and power of it all: the allure and the sweet seduction of the South. We are surrounded by it, like love.

My purpose, my niche comes in to view, blinding me with crystal clear clarity. I am now an example, a role model, a pioneer. For many I meet, I am the first gay person they have ever known. The responsibility is one I accept willingly.

Despite the biscuits that are starting to burn in the oven, I answer the telephone in the kitchen.

This time, it is a man. He says to me in a Southern drawl, "We have a very exciting offer for you. May I speak to the lady of the house?"

Amused, I return the question with, "I'm the closest thing to a lady that you will find in this house."

There is a moment of silence on the other end which is followed by a feeble, "Excuse me?"

"What are you selling? And make it quick. I've got biscuits in the oven."

The Long Ride Home

Traci Lynn

Growing up gay in a small suburb in Texas required a combination of guilt and deception. It didn't help that I'd been born to a Lutheran minister and a native Houstonian semi-socialite whose father was pretty much the "Big Daddy, Right Wing Oil Man." And, it also didn't help that I felt obligated to live up to every little expectation that this crew had for me whether imagined...or very real. But, as early as the first year of junior high school, the pressures of my budding sexuality were presenting hurdles that I hadn't expected, and ones that I knew most others my age weren't dealing with.

The moment I laid eyes on my sixth grade speech teacher was when the proverbial light bulb went off. She was smart, beautiful...and I could swear that she thought me "special." Wishful thinking, perhaps, but when you're in the sixth grade, the mind swirls with wonderful thoughts, and it seemed entirely plausible that this woman in her late twenties or early thirties could have feelings for an eleven-year-old. Traci was in love. I sat in her class hanging on every word. When she sat at the teachers' table at lunch, I made sure I was close by just so that I could gaze into those beautiful blue eyes. In a way, I guess you could say that I was stalking her.

I excelled at the speech tournaments, winning the best speaker awards, and made darn certain that I won the talent shows that she organized...simply for the prize of her hugging me at the end of each show, and looking adoringly at me with those piercing baby blues. I wanted to protect her, to comfort her, to gently touch her cheek with my fingertips. I was certain that these feelings weren't quite normal, but they filled me with such joy and serenity that I was determined not to let them disappear.

And then, disaster struck. My glorious teacher had an announcement to make to the class. I was on the edge of my seat. Was there another talent show? Did she have a trip planned for her best students (myself included, of course)? Was our mime troop going on an overnight stay to Dallas? (My heart swooned.) And then she held up a denim shirt with two sets of initials lovingly embroidered on the back, surrounded with colorful flowers. One set of initials was hers: A.B. The other set...wasn't mine. That's when the ball dropped and she announced her engagement...to a wonderful man. The whole room went black. As the other children clapped and congratulated her, I gripped the edge of my desk so that I wouldn't pass out. It was the end of a beautiful dream, and it truly broke my heart. So, I did what any preteenager riddled with guilt over these thoughts would do. I went steady with every boy within a ten-mile range. "That'll show her", I thought, as my heart sank through the heels of my feet.

My parents divorced, and my mother re-married after a short stint of dating. It was 1976, and we moved to the outskirts of Houston. We were in the "boonies" with horses and rednecks by the droves! The high school (where I was bussed 30 miles away) was a completely different environment. There the hallways were filled with jocks, cheerleaders, and preppy kids of all shapes and sizes, the girls all being a perfect "size 6."

As I dated the football team (never going farther than "first base"), I continued to have feelings for women—huge, glorious, deep feelings for women. When would this go away? I certainly couldn't tell anyone about my deep dark secret, not at this school, so I began reading anything I could get my hands on that included a lesbian relationship. Lillian Hellmann's *The Children's Hour* was the only play at the time that I knew of involving this sort of debauchery, these hidden feelings for another woman. Of course, we all know what happened at the end—the guilt-ridden one kills herself in the back room. One gunshot, no more guilt.

That wasn't an option for me, so I turned instead to the book *Once Is Not Enough.* Now that was a relationship I could get into! The secretive, sexy meetings between the two older women sent me reeling. The feelings I had for the Football Player Flavor-of-the-Month didn't hold a candle to the fantasies I would conjure up about my new English teacher, or the tall, slender girls I played volleyball with. I had to explore.

Being in the drama department gave me lots of opportunities. I befriended a wonderful boy who, though still denying his own sexuality, had "gay-boy" written all over his 501s. I was determined to recruit Everett as my gay club partner on a very top-secret basis. At 16, we started clubbing. A whole new world opened up for me. Girls kissing girls…boys holding hands…women who were much older than I, having been together for years, holding each other. Perhaps there was hope. I belonged here.

And then…the guilt. The fear—no—the terror of my mother ever finding out. The lies that I told her about where I was. The questions about why I broke up with Football Flavor-of-the-Month. My popular girlfriends who tanned with me on the weekends, and spent hours flirting with guys in the hallways; what on earth would they think? The Texas right-wing agenda being tossed into my face each and every day. And, of course, that's when I fell in lust…with Lynn. Filled with charm and rather exciting danger, Lynn looked like a sun-kissed California girl with perfect teeth and inviting dimples to decorate her beautifully tanned face. I had to have her. I had to try this out.

At the time, Lynn lived in a luxury townhouse with her "Mommy Dearest" and her younger brother. Because I still lived at home, we decided that the best way to "be" with each other was to sneak me into the townhouse when her Mother had "had a few," and make love in her bedroom, or the guest bathroom, depending on which part of the house in which "Dearest" was sipping that evening. On occasion, "Dearest" and I would run into each other and exchange niceties, though strained.

Because Lynn and I felt that "Dearest" was catching on, we devised a plan: Christopher. "Christopher" was the reason that Lynn and I hung out together so much. The fictional Christopher was my brother whom Lynn had a "thing" for, and, when the question arose from my mother, Christopher was Lynn's brother on whom I had a crush. (The fact that neither mom ever met the fictional stud didn't occur to either of us. We simply made him so "hard to get" that we settled for the company of each other, while "waiting" for

Chris to come around.) I even received a lovely bunch of yellow roses from my darling "Christopher," which my Mother promptly put into a Waterford vase for us to admire during dinner. Things were going along swimmingly until the dreaded phone call.

My (then) stepfather was a rather mild-mannered CPA. He was handsome, financially set, and loved to ski Aspen, which was just what the doctor had ordered for my mother at the time after her divorce from my father. We had a ritual, when I wasn't in rehearsal for a play, of his picking me up from my summer bank job (counting endless checks and filing them in these huge bins that looked like a Rolodex on steroids) and singing to Willy Nelson on the long ride home. Sometimes, he'd even pop open a beer as he drove Interstate 10, never thinking about driving while drinking. After all, this was Texas in the dawn of the 1980s. This became a rather pleasant occasion for me, and I often looked forward to these drives.

Then "the call" happened. I was playing the lead role in a wonderful play in downtown Houston. I often rehearsed after work three or four days a week during this period, and, if I was without my car, I would catch a ride with one of the other actors after the long, cherished rehearsals. It was around three in the afternoon when I received the dreaded phone call from my stepfather.

"Traci, what time do you leave work?" he said slowly.

"Um…five, as usual. Why?"

"I'll pick you up in front of the bank", he replied, with a tone I'd never heard from him.

"No. I have rehearsal, remember? We open this Friday. I'll see you at home later."

"No, you won't. I'm picking you up. Your mother needs to have a talk with you."

My mother needs to have a "talk" with me? What "talk?" Certainly not "the" talk. She'd had that chance a few years ago and skipped it. Life went on, and I learned about my period from my cousins and the girls at school. What "talk" could possibly be important enough to drag me out of an important rehearsal? I hadn't done anything wrong. I was a "good girl" almost to a fault. And, she couldn't possibly know about…(gulp)…or could she?

My pulse rate jumped through the roof.

"Um, Okay. I'll call Ted and tell him I won't be at rehearsal."

"See you at five," he barked.

"Is…everything…is this a family thing? Was there a death or something?" I said, hopefully wishing one of the older relatives had peacefully slid away from us and saved me from this possible disaster.

"Nope. This is about you. Be out in front at five."

The phone slid from my grip, as my palms were dripping with sweat. What time was it? Three? I have two more hours? How will I possibly survive these next 120, and then the added time of the drive home? Think, Traci, think! I'm seventeen, I thought. I can handle this. Besides, I'm not yet certain that she's found out about me. She's level-headed. We'll deal with this. As adults. That's right, two adult women. Unconvinced, I slid into my chair and tried to steady my hands as I went back to the mundane task of filing records of other people's money.

If you had peered into the car as we crawled along Interstate 10 that afternoon, you'd have thought we were headed to a funeral. I suppose, in some ways, we were. I was about to encounter the death of a part of my relationship with my mother. It was a pivotal moment in our lives, and the direction that we would go from here was up to her. The choice was hers.

As we pulled up the driveway, after the awful silence, sans Willy Nelson, sans his occasional beer, I noticed the truck with the workmen pulling away. My mother was, and still is, an amazing decorator, and we always had something going on at the house: building a new deck, redecorating the kitchen, new fixtures in the bathrooms. This time, we were retiling the entire downstairs living area with magnificent Mexican tile.

The dread began in my toes, and worked its way up to the hair follicles on my head. As we pulled into the garage, I heard what sounded like wailing. The sort of tearful wailing that you would expect if a young child had been hit by a car. Or, if you'd just found out that your son in the military had been gunned down.

This couldn't possibly be for me, I thought. I'm her successful girl. I was in the Honor Society, I had scholarship offers up the wazoo! I had been a top-notch student, an exceptional athlete, and an award-winning actress. I'd never been pregnant, and had only missed my curfew a handful of times, and that was because we lived so darn far from the city! My stepfather had made a mistake. This wasn't about me. Perhaps this was something terrible! After all, this expression of grief was far too dramatic, far too organic to belong to something as simple as a teen's sexuality.

As I entered the living area, and headed toward the master bedroom where my mother was in tears, I literally had to walk a plank. Because the floors weren't quite finished, the workmen had put a wide plank across the large room, so that we wouldn't disturb the newly laid tile. And, it was while walking across this plank that my dread was confirmed.

"Dick! Oh, Dick, your daughter is…is seeing another girl!" she sobbed into the telephone.

I don't know what shocked me more: that she'd "found me out", or that, after years of wishing he was dead, my mother chose to call my father!

I stopped for a moment to catch my breath before entering the bedroom. At this moment, for this sliver of time, a great calm came over me. She knew. There. That was that. I had no more secrets, and I was certain that we could work this out.

I walked into the room and saw my mother as I'd never seen her before. She was beside herself with emotion. There was a heap of used tissues next to her on the bed, and her eyes were so puffy, they almost looked closed. I gave her a small smile, and she grieved even more. She held out the phone as if to say: "Here, tell your father what I've just found out. Tell him about you."

I took the phone.

"Dad?"

"So, your mother found out you're gay, I hear."

"Yeah. Yeah…I'm sorry I didn't tell you. I'm sorry…"

"I've know that for years, Traci," Dad said with his soothing tone.

"Really?...I...," I was floored. Had he really known?

"I could have told you this ages ago!" he said, almost with a chuckle. "Trouble is, now you have to deal with your mom. Call me later. I'm here."

I hung up the phone, and, after a moment, looked directly at my poor Mother. As her sobbing began to crescendo, it dawned on me that she was truly devastated by this news. She was hurt. And, she was worried about me. I handed her another tissue in a futile effort to stop the crying. I felt the presence of my stepfather standing behind me, and realized that this was huge!

"This...will ruin your career!" she sobbed over and over again. "Lynn's...mother found...she read me a letter that you had written to...to...L-Lynn!"

Perfect, I thought. "Mommy Dearest" had called my mother, who actually was dear in her own studied way, to tell her how I had "seduced" her perfect daughter and taken her down the path of sordid lesbianism.

My stepfather bristled. I tried to explain, to no avail. It seemed to me, at that moment, that everything that I was before, everything that I'd accomplished and worked so hard to be, paled, faded drastically now that we knew who I really was.

"Mom, please, stop crying! I'm still me! I'm the same person who walked out the door this morning as we talked about the play opening this week! I'm the same girl that you were so proud of when I accepted the scholarship to U of H! C'mon, Mom. This isn't so tragic."

Apparently, I was mistaken. It was tragic…to her. There was no stopping her. The tears kept flowing, and the communication had now slipped into monosyllabic jibber. Again, I felt a distinct bristle from my stepfather.

"You have…you've really hurt your mother," he said with an uncharacteristic tone. "You've really done it, Traci. You really have."

His Texas accent seemed more pronounced than ever. The anger and sadness that filled the air was impenetrable. Any communication skills that I had learned in my years in the theater seemed to vanish. There was no moving forward here. We had reached the dark hole.

I had to leave. If just for a while, I needed to get out of this house, for everyone's sake. My mind raced to my younger brother who was upstairs in his bedroom listening to this horror. I needed to explain to him what was happening, and that I had to leave for a while. As I turned to walk out of the room, I felt an unmistakable heat from my stepfather's body. He was angry. He didn't know what to do, and he had to take it out on somebody. I walked past him, and went upstairs.

I opened the door to my brother's room and saw him sitting on the floor in the corner. He looked up at me with so much love in his huge brown eyes.

"What's going on? Are you okay, Trace? What's happening?"

"Scott," I said wanting to make everything right for him, "this is about me. I'm gonna take care of things, but I'll probably have to go stay with Dad for a while. This has nothing to do with you. I'll explain this some other time. I love you, buddy."

The door slammed open. Scott stood, knowing what was coming. My stepfather rushed into the room, furious.

"You have upset your mom to no end!" He screamed at me. "What do you plan to do about it?"

As he came toward the center of the room, Scott stepped between us in an attempt to calm him down and, I suppose, to protect me. I had never ever had an angry encounter with my stepfather. In fact, we'd had, up until that point, a pretty easy-going relationship. As I found out much later on, my brother did not share that experience with him. In fact, theirs was filled with violence and resentment that only a teenaged boy and his new stepfather can understand.

As Scott put himself between us, he was angrily shoved toward a wall, banging his head and upper back onto a large framed poster, sending it crashing to the floor.

"Stop it!" I screamed. "Just stop it! My god, why are you so angry? Why?"

I couldn't fathom what was happening. I could not wrap my mind around this turn of events. All in my honor. All because I had discovered that I was emotionally and sensually more connected with women than men. That I chose the softness of a woman's body, her smell, her tenderness over that of a man's. This seemed very simple to me. Something to be celebrated, not demonized, not made into something ugly.

Shamed, my stepfather slowly backed out of the room. I helped Scott up from the floor and, holding his hands, looked him squarely in the face.

"This is not about you. Do not allow him to push you again. Ever," I whispered, not knowing that it was a common occurrence.

"Okay. Love you, Trace," He said. "You call me and let me know where you are."

"I will, buddy. As soon as I know which way is 'up', I'll call you. I think you should probably chill in your room tonight, you know? Let things calm down. I'll explain this to you...soon."

"Love you."

"I love you, too, Scotty."

And, as I walked out of his bedroom and into mine to collect some things, that's when my tears began. They were slow, welled up, silent tears. My heart and my throat were swollen with sadness: sadness for my brother, for myself, and for what I suddenly was labeled today that I wasn't yesterday. Was I truly as bad as they thought? Was my mother right? Would this harm my career? Now that she knew, was everything good erased? Was there something inside of me that was so black, so damaged that nothing else mattered?

I packed a small bag, drove to a 7-11, and called my father.

In my mother's defense, I've often wondered what that day would have been like if things had been handled more carefully—if Lynn's mother had simply called mine to calmly discuss her daughter's relationship with hers. Having known this woman, I can only guess what venom must have been spewed in that short, angry phone call. I'm certain that my mother was taken off-guard, and truly upset. Therefore, shame on "Mommy Dearest." And, frankly, shame on any parent who doesn't "begin with the end in mind" and realize that the path of discussion that they choose is entirely up to them—that the choice made in those few moments, will affect their relationship with their child for years to come, if not irrevocably alter it forever.

Years later, on a visit back to Houston with my then-partner Sarah, I heard a tale from a dear friend and associate of my mom's who just happened to be gay. We were having a drink with Judy after mom had set us up to discuss where Sarah could go golfing in Houston during our visit. Golfing, in my opinion, is about as interesting as eating a cardboard box; however, I thought it might be enlightening to talk with this lady who was gay and had known my mother for so long. Sure enough, I was right.

We met Judy at a bar for a nightcap after having dinner with mom and sending her off, and there we sat, the three of us, shooting the lesbian shit at a gay club near downtown Houston. Yes, indeed, there were many places to golf that week, but Judy had a story that she really wanted to tell. As Sarah sipped her drink and daydreamed about hitting the links, Judy told me a story that gave me new insight into my mother.

Darling Judy had worked for my mother and, though for years she wasn't out with her because she was her employer, Judy had always had a soft spot for her, and wished that she could tell her about her lifestyle. On a business trip to Austin, Judy, Mother, and another associate were sharing a rather large suite. They each had their own bedrooms, which were connected to a shared living area within the suite. One evening, the three women were getting dolled up to go to a business dinner, and as my mother was putting on her makeup, she could hear the loud television in the connecting living area. That evening's blurb was about the Olympian Greg Louganis and his bout with AIDS. It seems that Judy and the other woman were having a rather emotional debate about this man and his sexuality when, as Judy remembers so vividly, my mother walked into the living area holding her mascara like a weapon. Pointing the innocent Maybelline toward the women, she announced in her soft Texas accent:

"I hope you're not speaking in the negative about Greg Louganis and his homosexuality. My daughter is gay, and I'm extremely proud of her."

There was a moment of silence, the mascara tube still pointing at the women. Then, Judy and the associate looked at each other and burst out laughing.

"So am I," Judy said.

"Me too," said the associate.

Apparently, there was shared a sigh of relief, a few chuckles, and then mom went back to the duties of applying her eye makeup.

Though my mother and I have successfully repaired our relationship, which was severed for many years, I can't seem to wash my day of reckoning from my memory. The day of my long ride home. For a while, it changed the way I felt about myself and my sexuality. There was always this little black mark somewhere in the deepest recess of my brain and my soul. There was a little voice which said: "No matter how genuine you are, how innately good you truly are, how talented, how smart...you're still gay. And they seemed to think that was the end of the world at one point."

Forgive ignorance. Forgive intolerance. But only when there is an effort to change, to grow, and to truly understand. Thank you, Dad, for always knowing that. And, thank you, Mom, for having the courage to make the effort to understand.

Loving Mountains, Loving Men

Jeff Mann

HINTON AND HEJIRA

Mountain Lake, Virginia, Summer 1998. I am teaching a course on Appalachian culture for Elderhostel students. A fine setting, this rustic stone resort high in the Alleghenies, and enthusiastic students, these retired folks much more eager to learn than many of my students at Virginia Tech. I discuss poetry by James Still and Maggie Anderson, fiction by Harriette Arnow and Lee Smith. Then I read a few of my own poems, the overtly Appalachian ones, the ones without gay references, the ones not likely to give offense. I can tell that they think I am a nice young man, and their image of me would be shattered, I fear, if they knew how fond I am of other nice young men.

For a break, I get out my dulcimer in mid-afternoon. As much as I want to spin out a fine yarn about how "this here dulcimer was carved by my granddaddy out of black walnut from the family farm, and he taught me all these songs when I was a child," today I confess to my audience that I am not some male Jean Ritchie, inheritor of rich oral legacy I discovered the dulcimer not through family or even regional tradition, but through the music of Joni Mitchell. This dulcimer, I gingerly admit, was a cheap mail-order version I bought long ago, when my undergraduate budget wouldn't allow me to buy the arts-and-crafts-fair home-built variety. The Elderhostelers are visibly disappointed.

After playing them a few folk ballads, I retune and play the dulcimer song I love the best, Joni's "A Case of You." The taste of Proust's *Madeleine* can evoke history, certainly, but, as has often been noted, so can a melody. Today I want to remember when I first heard the music of Joni Mitchell.

Not that day when this dulcimer was ordered from Elderly Instruments in Michigan my senior year in college. "Spruce top, mahogany back and sides," I used to chant to myself during that long walk from Lorenz Avenue to forestry classes at Percival Hall, dreaming of the day the instrument would arrive.

Not that evening in Cin's apartment when Will first showed me how to play "A Case of You," Will, the bearded, furry-chested friend of a friend whose sexuality was ambiguous enough to prevent me from making a pass, whose strong-armed hugs made me gasp and yearn for more.

Not those autumn evenings in the Fall of 1977 in Sunnyside, Morgantown's student ghetto, when Allen, the first gay man who ever befriended me, played Joni's album *Blue* again and again, and I first fell in love with the song's lyrical sadness.

What I want is further back. High school days, the time few gays and lesbians remember with fondness. My years at Hinton High School, in the mid-seventies.

*

It must have been the Fall of 1976, as far as I can gauge from this distance. Where did I find it, *Hejira*, the first Joni Mitchell album I ever bought? A local drugstore, I suspect. Up 'til then, I'd listened to the Carpenters, the Partridge Family, Elton John, Neil Diamond. But, to use the Southern phrase, I was, that autumn, "standin' in need" of more intelligent, more complex, more literate music to keep me company, to soften my loneliness and comfort my melancholy, to shore up my dreams of escape. "Hejira" means, after all, "flight or withdrawal from somewhere, especially to escape from danger." I stumbled upon Joni's haunting collection of travel-themed songs at a time when good books and moving music were almost all I had, when my emotional isolation felt almost complete, when travel to somewhere more welcoming constantly composed my daydreams.

What made this loneliness more piercing was that it followed months of queer camaraderie, the sweet siblinghood of misfits, a hard thing to find in southern West Virginia in any decade. I had had a circle of supportive lesbian friends, but that circle was for the most part dispersed by then. Jo had been forced to leave her teaching position at Hinton High by the homophobic principal, a man I detest to this day. Bill and Kaye, a class ahead of me, had graduated and moved on to attend West Virginia University, sending me letters about their discovery of a gay bar and the new queer friends they were making. I lived for those letters. They made me sick with envy, but they gave me hope. One day, I knew, it would be my turn to "get my gorgeous wings and fly away," as Joni put it. Till then, I was stuck in Hinton, West Virginia, to complete my senior year before fleeing to WVU myself.

Only Laurie remained, a younger lesbian who lived nearby. Every evening we met in the park and walked across a bridge recently built over the New River. No matter how cold the night, we sat on the concrete railing, watched the black water rush by below, discussed the unfortunately straight boys and girls we found attractive, and wondered how our distant friends were doing in the Brave New World of university life. Surely somewhere in Morgantown, I thought, I would meet an attractive man worth loving, a man who would meet my hot urge to touch with an eager urge of his own.

*

Hinton is an isolated railroad town along the New River. Then and now, about 3,500 people live there, most of them conservative and religious, most of them, I would imagine, hostile to gays. It is like many small towns in and out of Appalachia: It is dangerous to be openly queer there. To this day, as big and mean, bearded, booted, and leather-clad as I have become (look tough, and people are more likely to leave you alone), I feel ill at ease, paranoid, when I am in Hinton—especially now that I have published a good bit of openly gay material, especially now that my editorial-writing father has referred to my sexuality in his newspaper essays attacking fundamentalism and homophobia. As much as I muse on the warrior archetype, delight vicariously in handsome Aragorn's swordplay in *The Lord of the Rings* films, and relish the revenge fantasies allowed by writing and reading fiction, I realize that, in reality, I am outnumbered.

I was neither big nor mean when I met Jo, the teacher who was to become my lesbian mentor. I was a shy, quiet, plump, insecure, unattractive, bookish kid, with long, dark, rebellious hair, good Southern manners, and no sense at all of the warrior mentality that a hostile world would someday inspire in me. Jo, who'd been teaching biology at Hinton High for several years, had founded an Ecology Club in which my older cousin Ann participated. One day Ann, having decided, most probably, that I spent too much time studying, invited me along on a club jaunt.

It was, I think, a Saturday morning in the spring of 1975 that Jo and I officially met. Her blue Gremlin pulled up to the Forest Hill post office where I waited at the pre-appointed time. Ann gestured me inside, and off the three of us went, armed with a detailed road map to track down abandoned cars for A. James Manchin's REAP program. All day we bumped down rough back roads, knocked on doors, got permission forms signed, and spray-painted green thetas, the Ecology Club symbol, on those old wrecks the owners had agreed to let the state dispose.

Jo must have liked something about me, or recognized my queer potential, so to speak, because soon I was encouraged to become a regular member of the Ecology Club. During my sophomore year, I spent just about every Saturday working on nature trails, learning to identify trees, picking up roadside litter, or enjoying hot dog roasts with other club members. Eventually, I became one of an inner circle of students who hung around Jo's home on some Sundays, a home she shared with another woman, Robbi. Robbi was, supposedly, Jo's ward.

And eventually Jo came out to me. Inspired by a textbook controversy in Kanawha County, West Virginia, in which local fundamentalists had tried to control what textbooks might be used in public schools, she had begun writing The Colony trilogy, a series of novels set in a future controlled by Christian fundamentalists, long hunt-and-peck typewritten manuscripts that she let me read. In her fiction, free thinkers escaped this theocratic society and created their own hidden community, a colony in the Canadian Rockies. At one point in the second novel, two of the female characters, to my surprise, became lovers. In the third novel, almost all the main characters were lesbians. She was taking a great risk showing such material to a high school student in a small rural town—show such subversive texts to the wrong student, the easily shocked student with the big mouth and the devout parents, and you're liable to be run out of town. But she had judged her audience right. Raised by liberal parents on nonconformist treatises by Emerson and Thoreau, I responded only with curiosity and a desire for more information. I even asked if she had any books about male homosexuals. It was then that Jo lent me Patricia Nell Warren's novel *The Front Runner.*

*

Last May, I attended the first Saints and Sinners Literary Festival in New Orleans, an event featuring gay and lesbian writers. At the opening reception, a friend introduced me to Patricia Nell Warren, and I was momentarily speechless. How could I tell this woman, without a fan's awkward spluttering, how much her work had changed my life? I did my best—not my most articulate moment—and Warren kindly posed with me for a photo when my partner John, seizing the opportunity, whipped out his digital camera.

The Front Runner, published in 1974, was one of the first novels to deal intelligently, compassionately, and realistically with a male homosexual relationship. The narrator, Harlan Brown, describes his attraction to his star runner, Billy Sive, who's training for the Olympics, their eventual relationship, and the scandal it causes. Jo, in lending me that novel, saved me years of self-doubt, self-loathing, fear and confusion. I read that dog-eared paperback in only a few days, and when I finished, I'd fallen in love with Billy Sive, and I had begun to understand yearnings which I had always dismissed before as admiration or envy. I found a name for what some men made me feel. Unnamed, an emotion can stay inchoate, nebulous; it can sink back into oblivion. Named, a passion takes on force, meaning, depth, and direction.

What an indescribable and life-saving gift, the gift of self-knowledge. Sometimes it destroys, as it did Oedipus. In my case, it gave me first the rich camaraderie of exiles, those times spent with Jo and my fellow misfits of the Colony (as we called both our circle of friends and Jo's farmhouse). When those friends left town and the Colony dispersed, self-knowledge gave me bitter isolation and deepened my desperate yearning for a place and time far from Hinton, that scenic but intolerant mountain town. I learned the survival techniques of gay high schoolers: lies, omissions, subterfuge, protective coloration, a skilled peripheral vision with which to admire men on the sly. I read gay-themed novels to escape the all-encompassing straight world: Patricia Nell Warren's *The Fancy Dancer*, about a sexy, black-leather-clad hero who seduces a priest; Mary Renault's *The Persian Boy*, told from the point of view of Alexander the Great's young lover. I lay on my bed in the dark—traditional position of the alienated adolescent—listened to Joni sing "Refuge of the Roads" and dreamed of a day when my escape would be more than mental.

*

I escaped Hinton. I fled to Morgantown and West Virginia University, where I stayed for undergraduate and graduate schools. I found no magically welcoming gay paradise, no passionately reciprocal relationship such as that shared by Billy Sive and Harlan Brown. Only brief flings, shared lust, three or four unrequited loves, the smoke of shoddy gay bars. Setting my hopes on the larger arena of the big city, I briefly escaped Appalachia. I taught at George Washington University during fall semester 1985, was dismayed by the coldness of the faculty, the mercenary obsessions of city dwellers, and the constant irritants of urban life. At the beginning of the Christmas holidays, I rode Amtrak back through the slate-gray hills and hefted my luggage down off the train and onto the station platform at Hinton. The gay world had disappointed me, so I returned to the only place I knew. Somehow I would have to make my peace with home. If men could not love me, then I would learn to live without love. I would devote myself to the beauty of landscape.

*

"I could drink a case of you," goes Joni's song. I cannot sing it—the melody is far too complex for my untrained voice—but the Elderhostelers seem to enjoy the strummed dulcimer chords. The afternoon session is almost ended. Soon, time to walk around the lake. John will be done with classes soon and will drive up here to Mountain Lake for cocktails, dinner, and a night with me in the rough-stone lodge. What will the Elderhostelers make of him, I wonder. I am dark and he is light. We could not be mistaken for brothers.

EPHEMERA OF SKIN

January 2004, Huntington, West Virginia. John and I are gleefully battening on a Swedish smorgasbord, a benefit for a rape crisis center. I love Scandinavian cuisine. Close to my beloved German food in its weight and depth of flavors, and such a treat not to have to cook it myself, here in a state where good ethnic restaurants are few and far between. I am almost through my second precariously heaped plate of meatballs, pickled herring, potato salad, deviled eggs, and creamed cabbage when my hostess introduces me to Justen, a young man from Boone County. Shy, intelligent, handsome, Justen is leaving West Virginia within a few days, heading to Los Angeles to start an internship.

He's leaving in the nick of time, our hostess explains, because he was openly gay in his home county and now feels that he cannot return there safely. Justen was punched, insulted, and threatened by fellow high school students. He suffered from depression and contemplated suicide. Finally he fled Boone County and was informally adopted by a sympathetic gay couple in Huntington, where he continued his education in a more liberal environment.

As I sit there, sipping my glogg and engulfing rice pudding, I try to imagine being openly gay in my home county of Summers, now or back in the '70's, during my high school years. I think about all the omissions I managed, the lies I told, the many ways I shielded my true self from sight, and I shake my head. All my big butch passions for swords and Scottish dirks and leather jackets, cultivating my courage for twenty-five years, and this kid, a head shorter than I, this kid's bravery puts me to shame.

When, at evening's end, I hug him goodbye (gay men do a lot more hugging than straight guys), I'm hugging some gutsier version of the boy I was at his age, the kid hot to get out of West Virginia and make a home somewhere less hostile. Will he miss brown beans and cornbread, the local dialect? Will he miss the blooming redbud and sarvisberry in the spring, as I did? I hope not. I hope he loves Los Angeles. I hope he meets a slew of available men, finds a wide-ranging circle of friends, and I hope he stays.

*

Forgive me the fantasy. I assure you that, outside the purlieus of my dreams, I am relatively harmless. But daily life is rarely intense enough for my taste, especially now that middle age thickens about me. Reality so often seems inadequate and restrictive, so seldom accommodating free expressions of my lust and my rage. If one were allowed to choose what the ideal afterlife might be, paradise for me might be composed of two things. One, ravishing all the many, many men I have yearned for in life but never possessed. Two, wreaking my revenge on all those who have crossed me and those I care for.

Because it is fantasy, the laws of probability are entirely on my side. None of them has the guns that, in real life, would end my rampage within a minute. And because it is fantasy, I feel no ambivalence, no guilt, no fear of consequences, just pleasure. I swing the Aragorn sword—a good ten pounds' worth—and, one by one, off come the heads. Unlike the unseemly manic dance of decapitated chickens, these bodies simply slump to the ground, every one of those who mocked or harassed him. It's like a cornfield after the stalks have been cut and shocked: the stumps of the recently truncated. I wipe the rich blood off my blade, hum a murder ballad, then head over to the next county in search of another just harvest.

*

Justen, I am too much of a country boy to believe that Los Angeles is safe. Be careful. Stick to the gay neighborhoods after dark. Remember how fragile we are. Eat lots of Mexican cuisine for me, and good California seafood. Check out the bars and the beaches, and drop us an e-mail containing the most outrageous details. If you ever get back to these mountains, let me know, and John and I will have you up for dinner. Name the cuisine and cocktails of your choice. If you come home missing West Virginia food, you don't have to go back to Boone County to get it. Fuck Boone County, or at least those in Boone County who were cruel to you. Come here, and we'll feed you brown beans and cornbread, chowchow, wilted lettuce, new peas and potatoes, ramps and creecy greens, biscuits and gravy. You name it. All you have to do in return is tell us about the sexiest leather guys in L.A. and the most garish drag queens. We're starved for misfit color in these here provinces.

LOSS AND THE DAILY BISCUIT

Perhaps it would have been easier to turn my back on the Appalachian region if my father hadn't been such a native son himself. Ever since I was a reluctant child, he has been inculcating mountain values and skills in me. As soon as he can, he leaves his law office and heads outdoors. In spring, he's planting potatoes and corn; in the summer, he's harvesting bushels of vegetables (name it, he's grown it); in the autumn, he's chopping wood, mulching the gardens with fallen leaves, bringing home turnips and kale; and in the winter, he's reading book after book, listening to classical music much too loud, cooking up great meals based on the garden produce he's canned, and poring over seed catalogs, dreaming of next year's harvest.

When I first skimmed through the Foxfire books, I was surprised at how many tools I recognized and at how many folk ways my father still kept up. When I teach the section on material folk culture in the Appalachian Folk Culture class, I don't have far to go for show-and-tell artifacts: elderberry spiles my father used to tap sugar maple trees, a corn husker, and a maul my great-grandfather carved out of an oak sapling, all in one piece.

When I have faced some of my greatest losses, I think of my forebears, making do, living on only what they grew themselves, and I know I have had an easy life and have endured very little. When I savor my father's fresh buttermilk biscuits, I know that love between men is a thing often expressed obliquely. And when I walk the Forest Hill farm with my father—its great oaks, its weedy pond, its dilapidated barn and red cedar groves—I know this is a landscape I can never leave, because I am too much of his son to live anywhere else.

SUNSET OVER HINTON

What kind of life would I have lived had I stayed there? It's a moot point, because there are few jobs in that area, certainly none in my field, but still I wonder.

Before I met John, first as a student and then as an instructor at WVU and later as a teacher at Virginia Tech, I spent summers and school breaks in Hinton. It was good to spend time at home, to get a lot of reading done and home cooking devoured. The grass-cutting got to be tiresome, and I never much liked picking strawberries, but other garden chores were fairly pleasant, at least as research for poems, and for a time I got to be semi-competent with an axe.

But as fond as I have always been of my family, and as open with them as I was even then about my true nature,

I often thought of a line from a Bette Midler song during those extended visits home: "Nobody knows me, I've got no reason to stay." My gay friends were in Blacksburg or Morgantown, and the nearest gay bar was in Bluefield, a friendly but shabby place I didn't think was worth the drive. Once in a while, I would stay over with my friend Allen in Stanaford and we'd drive down the West Virginia Turnpike to Charleston's Grand Palace to dance and watch the gaggles of big-haired drag queens. Ever so rarely, my Beckley buddy Jim would come down for some late-night dalliance. Other than that, I had a taste of the isolation I would have been swallowed by had I stayed in Hinton. I read a lot, I watched a lot of television. Always, at the end of the academic break, I was ready to go back to Morgantown or Blacksburg. A man needs to be around his own kind. For queer Appalachians, family is of monumental importance, but it is not enough.

*

Gays and lesbians must make themselves. None of us are brought up prepared to be gay. What did I know of homosexuality before I met Jo and read *The Front Runner*?

My first big trip out West. I'm twelve and ready to accompany Nanny and Poppy out to Grand Junction, Colorado, to visit Nanny's brother Harry. My mother sees fit to warn me about certain men who might get fresh with me in public restrooms. (That would be one desperate man, to hungrily approach the acne-stippled, pudgy adolescent I was.) "Just knee them in the groin," she advises, "and then run."

My father is listening to my grandmother play piano in the living room. "I used to play piano pretty well," he muses, "before the war. My first piano teacher made a pass at me. I never went back."

Someone in junior high tells me that Rock Hudson and Jim Nabors are getting married. "That can't be," I think, thoroughly confused. "Two men can't get married."

Playground gossip has it that the slender and effeminate son of a certain teacher has been caught in a compromising position in the movie house restroom with a fat, retarded kid who's the regular brunt of high school mockery. I have no idea what shameful things two boys could do together. I am very young and have been carefully sheltered by my mother's Southern good breeding. My imagination is very, very limited.

An ecology club cookout at the roadside park, just the other side of the Bluestone River Bridge. Too much lemonade, so I head for the bathroom. There, scrawled on the walls, Summers County gay history. Invitations, certain measurements, a sketch or two. A phone number, a suggested date and time to meet. Desperate attempts at connection in a wasteland, made sordid by secrecy. "FAG!" someone else has inked into the wood as critical commentary.

*

This winter afternoon, my friend Cindy is in town for a visit. She and I are walking past the Summers County Courthouse, a huge red-brick turreted structure. I look like I usually do: beard, jeans, lumberjack boots, black leather jacket. She is more anomalous in this context, for she is dressed pretty much the same as I, with the addition of one of those short haircuts the lesbian community favors. Women in Summers County do not dress like this.

A pickup truck passes us. A guy yells, "Go back where you came from!'

I am no longer that defenseless pacifist from high school. I am a pissed-off queer. Without missing a beat, I shout "Fuck you!" and flip them the accompanying gesture. Cindy and I are ready to tear off some body parts. However, unlike that night years ago when I got my face punched, the truck does not stop and eject pissed-off rednecks. Instead, it continues on down the street.

I turn to Cindy, laugh, then with mock-pathos wail, "I am where I came from!"

*

Had I remained there I would have needed a black belt or a bodyguard. I could not stay, but I have not gone far.

HER KITCHEN'S SQUARE OF SUNLIGHT

Family versus "family." A basic conflict for the gay or lesbian Appalachian. "Blood is thicker than water," my mother always said, and when I was recovering from yet another handsome man's indifference, I used to agree with her. Much has been said about the Appalachian attachment to family.

But in the gay community, biological family is often something to break away from. Some of us do it to avoid rejection, afraid to tell the truth about ourselves and so creating a protective distance. Some of us are forced to leave our families behind in order to escape their sometimes violent reactions to our sexuality. I think here of the character Jules in Lee Smith's *Black Mountain Breakdown*, who has clearly cultivated a strong contempt for his family, home, and heritage as a defensive mechanism, a preemptive gesture, knowing how likely his own rejection as a gay man might be.

So we speak of Family as a substitute: the gay community in general. "Is he Family?" we ask. "Ah, nice to be among Family," we sigh, entering a gay bar after a day spent with straight people. More specifically, when we say "Family," we have in mind the gay and lesbian friends to whom we give the energy and devotion usually reserved for parents and siblings.

So many gays and lesbians have to relinquish one family for another. Often the choice is made for them by the screams of a father or the cold shoulder of a sister.

Blessed among queers, those of us with supportive families, those of us who do not have to choose.

*

My junior year in high school. I'm walking down the crowded hall on my way to typing class when I pass one of my name-calling nemeses near the auditorium. He's a good-looking kid, with a muscular, hairy physique—a man's body, not a boy's—which I can't help but admire. I hate him nevertheless. Because he's short (and thus, I must note with vindictive amusement, often wearing clunky shoes with big heels in an attempt to look taller), he only insults me when he's traveling with his pack of friends. As he is today. "Faggot!" he growls as I walk by.

Coached by my mother to ignore insults rather than avenge them, I stick my nose up in the air, walk faster, and pretend not to have heard the hated word or the snickers that follow it. It's then that my little sister appears out of the stream of students hurrying to their next classes. It's her first year in junior high, her first year in this school. She stands before my accuser, pretends to laugh with him for a few seconds till he's off his guard, then suddenly shoves her middle fingers in his face and shouts, "Fuck you! FUCK you!"

Dwarf-Boy's face cracks like thin farm-pond ice beneath a lobbed stone. My sister is bigger than he is. His jackal-horde nervously disperses—no one's going to hit a girl, for God's sake, and this one's enraged—and within seconds his big heels are clopping hurriedly down the hall.

*

Amy and I have so much in common. Our values are almost identical, the predictable mountain attitudes that Loyal Jones summarized so neatly in his essay "Appalachian Values." We love these mountains, we are attached to family, we do for ourselves, we both love to cook down-home Southern food, we regard mainstream America—urban America—dubiously. We hate the same things: bad manners, incompetent child-rearing, conservatives, spendthrifts, bigots. Common hatreds and common loves—what else makes a relationship? And, when it comes to our choice of spouses, the majority would not approve. Her husband is black. My husband is male.

Before John and I met, many dissatisfying years went by full of bitterness, complaint, and regret, when coming home was a wonderful break from my loneliness. My sister is a care-giver par excellence, and spending time with her, enjoying her meals and her conversation, seeing in her the same sort of country caring that my grandmother embodied, began to make of Hinton and its surrounding hills not a prison but a shelter.

REDEFINING HOME

In the early 1990s, abandoned by one lover and yet to meet another, I lived frugally in Blacksburg, Virginia, mustering my funds in order to escape as often as finances allowed: visits to friends in San Francisco and Washington, D.C., trips to Europe every summer. Unhappily single, I decided that the world would be my distraction. As much as I loved Appalachia, there were other sides of me that needed expression: the man eager to find what adventure he could in big-city gay bars; the lover of exotic food and novel landscapes; the scholar of European literatures and cultures, eager to visit the many countries he'd read about but never seen.

But always, after those cosmopolitan flights, I would return to Appalachia and to loneliness. I would fill my days and nights with work. I would stride across campus or lift weights in the gym, studying the handsome young men about me and longing for what I couldn't have. Unused, my sexuality existed in suspended animation, a bulb with its potential for petal and scent resting in earth, quiescent, waiting for the right season. I felt root-bound: my attachment to my native place seemed to be ruining any chance I had for erotic fulfillment or romantic opportunity.

Only luck and persistence have allowed me to reconcile those two sides, the gay man and the mountaineer. Teaching Appalachian Studies at Virginia Tech over the last decade has helped me immeasurably to appreciate a native culture that once felt like a cage. And meeting John has allowed me to relinquish much of the resentment I felt towards the region when I was single. Now, in my life and in my writing, I try to bridge the inconsistencies and gaps as much as possible, by redefining myself, my conceptions of community and of home.

*

I almost belong here, I realized the first time I attended the Appalachian Writers' Workshop, held every summer at Hindman Settlement School in Knott County, Kentucky. For someone as complex as I, "almost" is good enough. For five days I attended readings and workshops; I enjoyed country food in the big cafeteria; I sat on cabin porches playing guitar and sipping verboten bourbon, chatting with other Appalachian writers. Nevertheless, I felt a strange tension, the anxiety a spy or imposter might feel, or anyone who is not what he seems. I was a little startled when a journalist noticed the rainbow rings on my baseball cap and asked me for a gay perspective on the Hindman community. Suddenly, I worried if the word would get around, and, if so, if I'd still be welcome in the men's dorm. It was, fortunately, a paranoia that was to prove groundless. Country dwellers are not known for their liberal views on sexuality, but writers are.

*

As a young man, I unconsciously patterned myself after the mountain men I grew up around, as well as my fellow forestry majors at West Virginia University. In other words, in my self-making, I emulated the very men I secretly desired. Thus my beard, boots, pickup truck, flannel shirts and tattoos, a common look in the mountains, one that has fed many redneck stereotypes. Beginning as a form of protective coloration and camouflage that allowed the queer kid I was to blend in, it's eventually allowed the queer adult I have become to define my own form of masculinity—my own peculiar combination of the wild and the groomed, the rough and the refined—and to achieve some solid sense of self, some sense of where I belong.

But this sense of belonging can be a shaky construct, and I find myself an occasional outsider in both mountain and gay communities. In most urban gay venues, my country look and country values are far from admired. In Appalachia, I'm always wondering how my fellow hillfolk will feel about me when they discover that I, a bearded mountain man, am often attracted to other bearded mountain men. This conflict is just an extreme sort of what most of us ponder: Who would accept me for all that I am, even my shadowy, secret sides? It makes for painful rifts between what we are and what we appear to be. What courage it takes to suture public self to private shadow.

*

I almost belong here, I realized, standing with John in a corner of the San Francisco Eagle, sipping bourbon and watching bearded men in jeans, boots, and leather jackets slouching sexily by. Later, the feeling of comfort was the same, down the street at the Lone Star, a bar catering to Bears, a gay subculture composed of masculine, beefy, hairy men whose taste in partners runs towards the same. I've never fit into most mainstream gay bars, whose denizens are as unimpressed with my beard and boots as I am with their styled hair and designer clothes. But since age twenty, when I nervously slipped into Cy's, my first leather bar, a hole in the wall in Washington, D.C, and found the kind of man I wanted to pursue and the kind of men I wanted to be, I have known which gay niche is meant for me. For a long while, the belonging was brief, since for many decades such bars existed only in big cities where I was unwilling to live. Now, however, with the slow expansion of gay culture in the cities of Appalachia, I can remain in the mountains and still enjoy the company of gay men very much like me. When I watch Bears and leathermen march in the West Virginia Pride Parade every June in Charleston, West Virginia, I can't help but remember my youthful years of secrecy and isolation. Then I brim with amazement and gratitude, knowing that the Mountain State has, in this respect at least, changed radically for the better.

*

In order to achieve any sort of wholeness, we must reconcile what looks irreconcilable. Despite mainstream mockery and hillbilly jokes, I will keep my accent and cling to my regional heritage. Despite conservatives' attempts to outlaw gay marriage, I will value my relationship with John just as my heterosexual ancestors valued their marriages, and I will make that connection that many try to deny: The way I love is as valid as the way my forebears loved. John and I, at day's end, will sit down together to refined pleasures like martinis and Brie, then relish mountain delicacies like ramps, cornbread, fried green tomatoes, or pinto beans with chowchow. Those years of waste are over, those years unsure of my place both in the gay community and in the mountains. What difficulties that remain in living as a gay Appalachian are tensions from which I will learn, from which I will make art.

What I hope my writing will do is reduce that tension for others, those who might see themselves reflected here, those who might have the strength not to retreat into an easy simplicity but rejoice instead in a difficult complexity. These words are my attempt to do what my father does every summer when he fills the pantry with home-canned garden produce, those rows of pickled beets, corn relish, tomatoes and green beans: capturing the generosity of the earth, saving summer's gifts for hard times, preserving the past to feed the future.

THE SILVER IN MY BEARD

August 1977, and I'm packing for college, stuffing the suitcases my parents got me for my high school graduation present. Much to my mother's delight, I've cut off the long, hippy hair I've worn for years. I've also grown a beard: black, with faint red highlights, a legacy from the Irish blood, perhaps. The beard's a little patchy, but it will be enough to create a new image, to give a new impression when I get to Morgantown. I'm tired of being who I was in high school. I don't want to be a celibate scholar obsessed with getting straight As. I want to be someone else in college. My body and my heart are as eager for education, experience, and development as my brain.

College will be my first extended foray into the world by myself, so I have to take Joni Mitchell's travel album Hejira with me. And a copy of *The Front Runner*, just to reread every now and then. And my denim jacket, which I pull out of my bedroom closet. I shake it out, hold it up, and begin to fold it.

Then I notice the tiny holes in the back of the jacket, and I'm reminded of why I'm so eager to leave my hometown. When I read *The Front Runner* in my junior year, I discovered that the gay liberation movement had adopted the Lambda as its symbol. When my friends Bill and Kaye preceded me in escaping to WVU, they'd reported that many men in the gay bar there wore denim jackets. So I bought a denim jacket and asked my friend Sally to stitch a Lambda on it. She had laboriously done so, in lavender thread.

I wore that jacket to high school for a week or two before I realized that, if I could find out that the Lambda represented gay liberation, so too could others in Hinton. Suddenly that letter on the back of my denim jacket felt like a target, a bullseye. One night, with a pair of scissors, I picked all the threads out. The lavender Lambda disappeared, inch by inch. An act of cowardice, a self-maiming, a necessity.

Today, I take the jacket with me to college, just as a reminder of why I can never live in Hinton again. I want to find a place where I can be both safe and honest.

*

Today I am learning to be safe. Today, George "Dubya" Bush has announced his support of a constitutional amendment opposing gay marriage, and I am attending a meeting of the Virginia Tech Boxing Club for the first time.

I haven't done anything even resembling this since the late 1970s, since those three Phys Ed classes in college—self-defense, karate, and aikido—none of which I was particularly skilled in. In fact, I used to joke to undergrad friends that I'd learned just enough of the martial arts to make myself dangerous to myself. From Sensei Boyd, I learned how to brandish a fistful of car keys, how to punch and kick, how to roll, how to dance through a few katas, but the practice, after those classes ended, lapsed into theory and fading memory.

For years—despite my hot temper, despite the semi-reasonable paranoia that being queer in America inspires—I have been putting it off, this fresh attempt to learn how to protect myself. Between teaching, traveling back and forth between Blacksburg and Charleston (with occasional weekends with my family in Hinton), and trying to write, revise, and publish, I have barely enough time to get to the gym to lift weights with any regularity. True, I've talked to a couple of black belts about perhaps taking some private lessons, I've read information about martial arts classes here in Blacksburg, and I've read a few books on the warrior archetype and relished a lot of action movies. But I'm still the leather-jacketed, booted, hillbilly/queer English professor who's good at striking a brooding, gray-bearded-biker pose (patchwork quilt of carefully constructed identity, masculinity as defensive barricade), but doesn't have much of an idea of how to implement his anger, of how to protect himself, his family or friends by kicking some attacker's ass if circumstances demand it. "Open up a can of Whoop-Ass," as my students put it. It's an expression I savor.

I have taught at Virginia Tech, as a fairly open gay man, since 1989, but only recently have I felt threatened. First, Karen was hired for an important position at Virginia Tech. But her lesbian partner, Shelli, was at the last minute refused a spousal-hire position by members of the Board of Visitors. Several months later, the board removed gays and lesbians from the lists of groups protected against discrimination on campus. The public outcry was so loud that the BOV relented, reversing both actions.

But now I am working for tenure, publishing lots of queer material and even some gay erotica. Some swine has complained to Virginia Tech alumni chapter presidents about the openly gay nature of my website, and the president of the United States has declared his opposition to gay marriage. I am anxious and I am angry, and my boyfriend has bought me a punching bag and gloves for Christmas. I want to learn how to use them.

The boxing coach is a friendly man with a thick local accent who makes me entirely welcome, even though, with this silver-streaked beard of mine, I am clearly out of place, over twenty years older than any of his other aspiring boxers. The kids adore him, it's clear. He knows all their names and asks about their lives as he wraps up their hands and helps them on with their gloves.

I watch a while—admittedly admiring a few young bits of scenery. (To adapt a phrase of mine, "I'm ethical, boys, I ain't blind!) Coach finally gets around to wrapping and gloving me, then gives me some basic directions—"Turn your hands this way. Okay, that's good. No, now, keep your hands up! Twist your wrist about here. It's the torque that produces the power..."

Waiting for my turn on a bag, I study the young boxers' efforts, trying to learn what I can from guys who obviously know what they're doing. Lots of muscular, athletic-looking white guys, of course. But, unusual for mostly Caucasian Virginia Tech, there's quite a multicultural mix in this room. A few Asian-American boys, a few African-American boys, a couple of African-American girls, a Middle Easterner or two. Plus a decent number of white boys who are small-framed or short. Then there's me, the German/Scottish/Irish/English-American queer. I wonder how many of these kids come here for the same reason I have: because they might feel a little marginalized, a little at risk.

Then it's my turn on the punching bag. Five two-minute rounds, one one-minute round, then thirty seconds of constant pummeling. I dance around the bag, trying to implement the coach's advice, hoping I don't look entirely foolish, entirely incompetent (every man's worst nightmare). I'm slamming as hard and fast as I can and imagining their faces—the hateful preachers and politicians, gay-bashers past and future—muttering "Son of a bitch!" under my breath.

"Work! Work now!" Coach shouts, and I punch even harder, determined not to look weak or lazy in front of these built young men, who are jumping rope or working their own bags and so probably not even noticing me. In between rounds, I sweat and suck in air, a little light-headed, hoping I don't faint or have a heart attack, regretting every extra Yuletide-, Candlemas-, or Valentine's Day-inspired belly-inch, wishing I'd come to this sport twenty years ago. How much different might my life have been with the underlying security and the daily physical confidence this sport surely provides?

Coach yells, "Relax!" but that—and pacing myself—will come later, with any luck and persistence. Right now, I'm going for strength, not speed or skill. I want that bag to swing crazily. I want to break through that carefully inculcated barrier that civilization palisades around each of us: "Don't hurt, don't break. Rein in." I want the strength and skill to protect what I love and to destroy what needs destroying.

*

A rainy autumn day, and John and I are visiting my family in Hinton. Daddy shows me his new conservative-skewering editorial, Amy tells me about her new court case, and I preen about my latest published poem and my boxing semi-prowess (always, always, the son's attempts to make the father proud). John sits quietly, observing the family dynamics he's grown accustomed to after our years together. Only my mother's absence makes the scene incomplete.

This afternoon we're transferring to the basement innumerable jars of produce that Daddy and Amy have canned. Later, we'll have a fire—John loves a wood fire, and Lord knows I've had enough practice making them, though I might have to split some kindling first. This evening, I'll start a new novel by Edmund White, one of my favorite gay writers, or get some Appalachian Studies class preparation done, or maybe waste some time finger-picking a few Tim McGraw or Joni Mitchell songs on the guitar.

Now, as we fill boxes with canned vegetables, I think about how much I enjoy returning to Hinton to see my family and to admire the beautiful landscape, the conjunction of mountains and river and sky. I think about how much I've changed, how much my hatred of the region has diminished and how much my love and my confidence have grown. Home, once the place I fled, has become the place I come to flee the world. A change well worth the silver in my beard, the furrows in my brow, my increasingly weighty history. It is the blessing of hardship, this deepening appreciation of kin: facing adversity side by side, passing sustenance hand to hand, creating safety and shelter against whatever cold may come.

A Womanly Thing

Esther Willison

"Coming out" seemed to me a teenaged term which I would never use for myself. But I use it now. With pride. I talk about my coming out because I do it every day of my life: to myself, to others, in my waking and sleeping, in my writing and reading. And someday, my death will come out of my life, and more will come out about me long after I am silent. I am not so egotistical that I foresee no end—but the end of my coming out might be the beginning of someone else's.

Those of us who have lived a secret life, for whatever reason, always marvel in the surprise of honesty, the ease of expression. We are amazed at the soft shape of our fears, their light weight and pleasing texture when we hold them in our hands and take a good look. Their appearance is not too different from other people's fears. What a discovery! Yet the coming out never ends because of the leftover staying in.

I cannot remember a time when I was not drawn to women emotionally, intellectually, and physically. The first two were easy; the last I had to hide. I had kept those feelings locked up for so long that, once freed, every vision of womanliness was a whole celebration, whole because it encompassed my mind, my emotions and all my senses. Looking at a woman's covered breasts is one of those celebrations, although it isn't only her breasts; it's when she's wearing clothing with folds or ripples, like a blouse, that follow the curves of her breast, that gentle echo of shape. It's a feminine hint as much as a sexual one. It's the delicate curve, the way the clothing comes around the breast or doesn't come around the breast; it's a womanly thing. It's the uneven quality of the way the blouse falls, one side a little more open than the other. There's still some fear of these pleasures, some slight guilt, as well as the joy and excitement and the laughing at myself, at catching a glimpse of a woman's bosom and finding it wonderful.

It's difficult now to go back and try to conjure up those feelings—the feelings I had in the closet. For one thing, when I was in high school, I never considered my homosexuality an option. It was like an illness, like the Epstein-Barr syndrome, where you're always tired and never well.

I grew up in Riverdale, New York, an affluent community in the Bronx. We were not so affluent, however, even though we lived that lifestyle. My parents rented a large apartment on the seventh floor of The Richmond House, an apartment building on Greystone Avenue, just a few blocks east of the West Side Highway and, farther, the Hudson River. No matter how normally I lived my life—boyfriends, movies, books, dances, synagogue on Friday nights—no matter how pretty I was, the illness was always there. I keep trying to compare it to something physical, because it is so physical. I was either trying to keep my longings at bay or I was fighting off the nausea that came with the attraction to other girls. I learned to live with it the same way you adjust to a limp: Your other foot does all the work.

It's not that I didn't like boys. I did. I went to a small private school in Riverdale, my brother and I both on scholarships. We walked to school, kicking stones to each other or picking up friends along the way. Everybody was "safe" in the early 1940s. Some of my best friends were boys: Billy, Chrissy, from the age of five. I wonder if that's because my brother and I were such good buddies. It doesn't matter. I enjoyed boys' company. I just didn't know how to have any physical feelings for them. And I knew it was a failing on my part. I wasn't repulsed. Not at all. Especially if I knew the boy well and felt at home with him. It was like nothing, like kissing a post. That's a cliché, but it fits perfectly. It wasn't even a personal insult to the boy; it was just a fact.

I remember kissing Margie on the mouth when I was eight years old. We used to play prince and princess out on the tiny balcony of her brownstone in the East Bronx. Her mother's name was Sid. I was curious about her mother because she had a man's name. (I don't think I knew about the name Sydelle back then and she was somewhat masculine looking.) When we got older, Margie and I double-dated. She went into a bedroom with her date while I lay on the floor in the living room with mine. I don't know where her parents were. My date was large, even fat—he looms as huge in my mind now, but I don't know if that's true. And he had a name I hated, like Ken. I let him reach into my dress and feel my breast. But I was so unresponsive, he stopped. Actually I don't know why he stopped, but that might have been the reason. We sat separately, he on the couch and me on a big chair, and waited for Margie and her date to reappear. Then he took me home. I never saw him again. I still feel angry with myself for being so passive. I understand why I was, but it doesn't help now.

My best friend all through grade school was Chrissy, a tall, skinny blond kid I adored. He liked me too, in a girlfriend way. He told me when we were older, but I don't think I ever knew that then. I loved and trusted him then, and still do. He is on staff at *The New York Times* and we still see each other once in a while. Now I'm crazy about both him and his wife.

I also developed a friendship with my fifth grade teacher. I guess it was what people call a "crush," but I never envisioned anything romantic. Instead, she and I began to fantasize about being famous scientists together and we called each other "Professor." The summer after fifth grade we wrote to each other, "Dear Professor, Here is a diagram of my newest discovery...." No matter how outrageous my letters were, she responded as if they were real. I made some calls to find out about her recently and found out she had lived with another woman and was indeed, a lesbian, and that she had died not long ago. I was amazed and not amazed. Amazed that I knew even then, but not amazed to know she was a lesbian. I was glad I had written to her some years after I was married, and she wrote back and sent me some drawings I had made for her in fifth grade. The drawings were so stiff and formal. I remembered them as much more imaginative. I wish I had gone to see her.

In middle school, I always had a boyfriend. Now that I think about it, it was as if I was extremely busy making sure I did always have a boyfriend. My prettiness and easy manner helped, I'm sure. Richie was my boyfriend for two years. We were great dancing partners, voted the best by our class, and we both loved going to the movies. We were quite compatible until he wanted to kiss me on the mouth. We broke up over that. How could I, later, let Ken feel my breast when I wouldn't even let Richie, at age twelve, kiss me on the lips?

After Richie, my boyfriend was Michael, a short, dark haired strikingly handsome boy with full lips and rosy cheeks. And a husky voice. Michael's best friend was Joel, who was my best friend's boyfriend. So in high school, the four of us—Andy, Joel, Michael and myself—were inseparable. In 1962, at my tenth high school reunion, Michael and I came out to each other. I always thought we pretended to do all the other things couples did, like petting, but didn't. He said, no, we did them, but we didn't enjoy it. And we both knew we weren't having a good time but didn't exactly know why. Michael and I became friends again. We wrote to each other and saw each other occasionally in New York. I used to stay in his apartment on Hudson Street. On one of those visits, he told me about his experience in high school, with Mr. L., one of our French teachers. He said Mr. L. had sexually molested him, and that he had been frightened but didn't know what to do about it. He liked Mr. L. but knew it was wrong to perform sexual acts for him. Looking back, Michael was angry with Mr. L. but felt it was too late to do anything. He had no idea where he was and didn't want to find him. I understood that, but my anger at this man remains. What a cruel, unforgivable thing to do to a young boy. Michael died of AIDS in the winter of 1994.

Towards the end of high school, my boyfriends were usually a year or two older. My last year in high school I fell in love with a friend named Rivka—I should say we fell in love with each other. For months, this meant just staring at each other longingly. We both knew but we couldn't talk about it, and we sure as hell couldn't act on it. Then, one evening, Rivka came over to my house to help me baby-sit. I lived in an apartment house in the Bronx, the seventh floor. Anne and Max lived on the third floor and we baby-sat for their son, Arnold. After he went to bed, we sat close to each other on the couch in the living room. We held each other for a long time and finally kissed gently. The whole thing puzzled us. "Who should be the boy?" Rivka asked. I didn't know. We shrugged our shoulders and kissed again. I started sleeping over at Rivka's house. She lived along Central Park West on 72nd Street. Her mother gave us her bedroom and she slept in Rivka's room, in her single bed. They had little money; her mother was a school teacher. Her father had died a long time ago; Rivka was maybe five when he died. I don't remember.

Together in her mother's bed, we were afraid. Hot, flushed, our hearts beating wildly, full of passion, we were tentative. We knew it was wrong. We knew we were sick. We knew no one could find out. Rivka had a boyfriend, Dirk, a tall, light-haired handsome boy, quiet like herself. And my boyfriend, Michael, was also handsome, as I mentioned before, dark and handsome. We were never jealous of each other's boyfriends. It was as if they were a necessity, like a coat in the winter or a racket on the tennis court. We never questioned them. And no one ever questioned us.

I told my best friend, Andy, that I loved Rivka. Andy was the only one in whom I ever confided. She was going to a psychiatrist for her own emotional problems, and she gave me his name. "Just have a consultation," she said. "It'll only cost ten dollars." I saved up ten dollars and dialed his number several times but never waited for a voice. I just couldn't do it. My "disease" scared me more than anything else I had ever known or could even think of. You know, learning to live with a secret is unbearable, terrifying; you are looking at people looking at you to see what they see, to guess what they know. And you are trying to act normal the whole time, casual, emphasizing your normality every chance you get; boyfriends, dates, dances, lipstick, bras... you name it, I talked about it. But after a while, once the secret is lodged in your chest, like that apple lodged in Gregor's breast in Kafka's *Metamorphosis*, you can't do without it. You need it to survive, you treasure this ghastly bulk, you look down to see it it's sticking out, and if it is, you shove it back in. You hold on to it; it's yours, nobody else's. You can't give it up.

Rivka and I went off to separate colleges, but we kept in touch. I used to call her when I got into Penn Station in New York on vacation. Well, we'd ask each other, are you over it? Did you meet a boy? Is it okay now? It was as if one of us had a disease that the other had contracted, and it was just a matter of time before we would be cured, each waiting for the other to get well so we would at least know that it was possible. But it never worked. And towards the end of the year, when I had called from the station just before going back to college, Rivka's mother told me that Rivka wasn't well. A nervous breakdown, she'd said. Best for her not to have visitors. I knew the disease must have taken a turn for the worse. Would that happen to me, I wondered? I wanted to go visit but didn't dare. Maybe it was my fault. I didn't call again.

My first year in college I became fascinated by Catholicism, and I spent part of each day that whole year praying for Jesus to send me a sign that he forgave me my illness. I listened so intently I thought my ears would fall off. I neglected studies, I went to mass, I saw Father John, the college priest, and I listened. But not a word. I gave up. My mother discovered a note from Father John (I use that word kindly, as she "discovered" it in my dresser drawer) and she dragged me to the Community Rabbi to talk. I told him I needed to be forgiven and then was terrified he would (or did I want him to?) guess my secret. I did learn, however, to keep my notes in school. But even now I have some left over churchliness. I am drawn to churches like a magnet. I sit in the back and look up at the ceiling, at the murals, if there are any, or at the figures in the front, or the stations of the cross on the side. And I wonder. I am filled with awe and curiosity at the story of Jesus. I never pray and I consider myself an atheist. But the smell of incense and the sound of Gregorian chants still give me a haven. I believe in grace, although I can't define it for you. I am drawn, as well, to my own heritage and I love the sound of Hebrew prayers, the lilt of the language and the splendor of the Torah being removed from the Ark.

These days I get angry easily. Not just at gay and lesbian injustice, at racial discrimination, at the bombing of Kuwait, at the invasion of Iraq. I inherited what's now called a "social conscience" from my parents. But I have a second-generation social conscience. I live well, travel, buy a convertible and go out to dinner. I'm not only out; I'm out and about. So there is the same conflict about being out when so many people are still in as there is about having enough money to live comfortably when so many people are barely surviving.

I met Malcolm at the end of my junior year, and I liked his easy manner. He left that year to help build the railroad in Nova Scotia. I wrote to him a few times but he never answered. A safe relationship. At the same time I hung out with a kind of folksy group, Phillipa and Ellen, girls who played the guitar and dressed boyishly. Ellen fascinated me. We made love once, a passionate but frantic exchange. I was sick afterwards.

Malcolm and I started seeing each other in my last year of college. I trusted him and was able to tell him, as I had told Andy four years earlier, that I was attracted to other girls. I told him about my relationship with Rivka. He was sympathetic, non-judgmental. Even understanding. He said a lot of people in high school have a sexual relationship with a friend. He said it's all a part of growing up. It wears off, he said. We outgrow it. I didn't know that and was so relieved. I asked him if he ever felt an attraction to another boy. He said yes, as a matter of fact, he had been attracted to his closest friend, H. But he knew it was just a phase of sexual development.

But it didn't wear off. I went to a psychiatrist one year after Malcolm and I were married and told him I didn't enjoy sex with my husband and that I was attracted to other women. He said, "You're making a mountain out of a molehill. Just do it more often and you'll learn to enjoy it. You're certainly not a homosexual. Don't worry about that." I was relieved to hear that and went home to wait for the change.

Malcolm and I moved to Schenectady, New York, in 1967. He was an instructor at Union College, and I was a homemaker with two daughters, Andrea and Judith. We eventually found a small apartment a few blocks from the college and I became a respectable "faculty wife." Schenectady is not a typical college town as it has (or had at that time) General Electric, which was the town's main financial support. But it was a conservative town (even more so now) and I was quite willing to play my role.

In the 18 years we were married, I fell in love with other women four times. The first three never knew (I don't think). The fourth woman, Far-out, I talked to. I told her I was attracted to her. She was straight but sympathetic and compassionate. Without knowing it then, I had already shifted a little. I was beginning to recognize my unhappiness, although I still knew I could never leave Malcolm. Marriage was sacred. Not in the religious sense, but in the moral sense. You married. You stayed married. No matter what, divorce was wrong. My mother told me that and it stayed with me. But even the slight shift, even the admission that something was amiss, enabled me to tell my friend, Far-out. She was young and open.

I met Faye, or Far-out, as I call her, in 1969. She had just finished college. I was thirty-six years old. She was a first-year teacher in our local high school. I worked part time in the high school, tutoring non-English-speaking students. I tutored some of Faye's kids. Before we met, we exchanged notes in our school mailboxes. Once she realized I was critical of the school system, she sent me this note: "You're like a lump on the breast of Public Education," with a drawing of a breast with a lump on it. I loved it and made a point of meeting her. We became friends and started out on our many years of adventures together, from smoking pot to dealing with cancer. She was (and still is) an artist, an adventure seeker. When we traveled in her "Motherbus" (VW van) with her German Shepherd, Caleb, it didn't matter if we drove one block or fifty miles. Everything we did together was unfettered. Far-out introduced me to the part of myself I had hidden along with my secret. She allowed me, encouraged me, taught me, tutored me in the art of living. So I trusted her, and I told her. And, in the telling came the relief of no more secret, the dissipation of my desire (although never the disappearance) and our friendship which is, after thirty-five years, still intact.

The point is not how many women I fell in love with. The point is what enabled me to finally admit my love? How did I go from being that self-hating girl who needed Jesus to forgive her to an outspoken dyke? How the hell did that happen? I have a theory which evolves in my mind like a train on the tracks. First the engine, so I could get it going, then the next car and the next, and the next until the caboose could take its place. Then the train went backwards, tightened the connections, then it stopped. Then, only then, could the engine start up again and be sure everything behind it was connected. Only then could the engine get going, be sure that the whole train was moving, really moving, along that track.

I left Malcolm in 1974 and, after a period of mourning my marriage, Far-out and I were relatively carefree. For a while I was in limbo—I wasn't straight and I wasn't gay. I was neutral. My old life was dead, but I wasn't ready for a new one. I was happy with my girls. I was happy having a close friend to share fantasies, to share unrequited love (for Far-out, a priest; for me, a married woman).

Far-out went away for a year to live in a commune in California. That was the year I helped to start an ungraded alternative or "free" public elementary school, The Open School. Getting the school going was an enormous amount of work: The school board had to grant approval, we had to find a building, hire the staff, invite the kids. It was work we welcomed. When the doors opened, we were a tight-knit group of ten people, our hearts beating wildly, our faces flushed with excitement and fear. I discovered something inside me I hardly recognized, a kind of creative strength. I learned change was possible.

The changes in my life were like those train cars, all connected to each other and to my coming out. But the coming out was as much about rising up as it was about moving forward; as much like a house was it is like that train. I laid the framework and before I knew it, the walls were up. And now it needs constant repair. Coming out is never a *fait accompli.*

Before I made the decision in 1974 to leave Malcolm, I called Rivka after twenty years of silence, and we saw each other. I wrote a fictionalized short story about that weekend. It's tempting to simply insert it here and go on from there. But that's the easy way out. And it's cheating. Besides, I've discovered that my fiction, compared to my non-fiction, is dull. All the words sound rounded, in the same way you would sand the corners of a box. My fiction is painted over to cover the grain. The words look nice, they feel smooth, but they're all alike and they run into each other to form a long, uninterrupted line. My non-fiction, imperfect as it is, runs rough. There's been no sanding. The sharp corners jut out, interrupt the flow. There's no paint to hide the flaws.

So here it is in non-fiction. (That's a misnomer also, because most of our memories are inaccurate—so at least some of what we remember is made up even if we're not aware of it, thus, the often contrasting recollections of siblings.) I visited Rivka when I was 39 and living in Schenectady. My daughters were fourteen and ten years old. I spent the weekend with her, in bed most of the time. I was both delirious and terrified on the way home, having experienced a kind of rebirth (sexually and womanly) and knowing I'd have to hurt my husband/best friend beyond belief, knowing how disturbing divorce is for kids. Wondering if I could do it. And I did. And it was even worse than I imagined. We cried together, he said stay and see women if you have to. I said no. And then the impossible part, after we separated, the coming out into a community who knew me as the straight married mother of two. And that, luckily, was easier than I had imagined. One friend told me to date another man, maybe he just wasn't the right one. Another asked, "Why did you get married? Why didn't you tell him before?" as if I was able to understand it myself. But most people said, "Okay, so that's it, eh? Well, waddya know?" Even my younger daughter, Judith, said, "You like women? Ugh, that's dizzgustung, but you're still my mom and I love you. But I'll never do that!"

I knew I needed the support of the lesbian community, but I couldn't ask for it. My close friend, Jackie, offered to go with me to the Women's Building for "counseling." She was supportive of me all along the way, supportive and realistic. The latter is something I'm not good at, although I've had to improve through no choice of my own. Jackie told me, "After you leave Malcolm, you may or may not be able to make a new relationship with a woman." I couldn't have come out without her help; she literally had to finish my sentences for me when we went to the Women's Center: "I think I'm a....." [long pause] "lesbian," Jackie added. The Center did counseling according to your income, and mine was small, because I had just starting teaching and the year was 1974. I believe I was making $7,000 a year with two kids and no child support, so my counseling fee was $3.00 an hour and I was eligible for food stamps. Without Jackie, I'd still be suffocating in the closet.

As my personal life began to develop, I was like an adolescent, going to the one hidden lesbian bar in the local area, picking up a woman once in a while, and being amazed at how comforting and easy it was to be with women. I had no luck with lasting relationships, though, until I met Barbara in 1981, just when I had given up. Barbara and I are as different as Vivaldi and Van Morrison. We did share, however, a fanatical desire to protect the rights of school kids. When she asked me out I said no because I'm 22 years older than her. I had to show her my driver's license to prove it. "Besides," I said, "when you're thirty-five you'll leave me for a younger woman." The night before her thirty-fifth birthday she woke me up to tell me, jokingly, "I'm leaving you tomorrow." But she was right. We were perfect for each other—and it turns out "older" is another one of those labels that peels off easily and has nothing to do with reality. Barbara is outspoken, honest, and unwavering in her love and devotion. I lucked out after all those years. At that time, however, we were both in the closet at work, afraid, again, of the narrowmindedness of our school community. She is also a teacher and, at that time, had a special education classroom with one aide. But one evening, after showing Barbara's aide around our house, (This is MY bedroom, this is Esther's bedroom.) we said to each other, "Let's never do that again!" What a relief.

Barbara and I have been struck down together with illness and tragedy and we're still moving in the same direction. It turns out that those experiences bring us closer and we have moved into a way of life where we give each other our best. That doesn't exclude fights, of course, just in case you think I'm romanticizing grief and loss and love and pain.

In the school where I taught in the late eighties (I was by that time in a conventional setting), everyone was fine with my "alternative lifestyle" as long as I didn't talk about Barbara as a spouse. For example, when the female teachers compared the sleeping habits of their husbands, if I mentioned Barbara in that context, I could clear the faculty room in three seconds. Two teachers in the closet came out to me—that was delightful. When I applied for a special job in the school system, I had to submit my portfolio (including my short stories) to the school board. A friend on the board advised me to exclude any story that had a gay person in it if I wanted the job. The coming out story I mentioned was in my portfolio. I'm embarrassed to say I took it out, and I got the job. I'll never know, will I?

So my workplace in Schenectady wasn't exactly safe, but it wasn't against me either. When the kids in my class called each other "faggot" I could ask them what that meant and let them know, or draw out from them in a discussion that there was nothing wrong with two men or two women loving each other. (The latter method was preferable.) I had the freedom to do that. When we had a parent gathering, if one parent told me Suzie's older brother was gay and had AIDS and then asked me if Suzie ever talked about it, I could tell her eventually that I, too, was gay. I always used the term *gay*, by the way, which seemed less alarming to people than *lesbian*. Among my own friends, straight and gay, I use *lesbian*, or *dyke*.

Now, after 23 years of being together, Barbara and I are an old married couple in our community. We're pretty quiet in the neighborhood, we don't fly a rainbow flag (we used to), we don't hold hands when we go for a walk, and we rarely go to marches anymore. Our political activities—both pro-rights for gays and lesbians and our anti-Bush activities—are either through the mail, over the Internet, or in small groups. We pretty much fit into the conventional middle-class lifestyle. I don't know how our neighbors would feel if we were outspoken activists with our names in the local newspaper every other day. (Can you tell part of me regrets we're not?)

I'm retired from teaching now and work in a small, independent local bookstore. The staff is mostly part-time, so there are many of us. I am the only dyke (that I know of). They are a diverse selection of young and not-so-young women, all with their own personal hardships. And all of them have welcomed myself and my spouse with intense warmth and openness.

It turns out what most people really care about is *not* your sexual orientation but your generosity, your respect for others, and your kindness as a human being. Call me naive but I live in a relatively small community and I feel safe, at home and at work. I recognize, of course, that as a homosexual, I am not safe in the larger picture, as long as I don't have equal rights and as long as there are people with hate in their hearts for "deviants" like myself. I try to put some energy into changing both of those realities. When I was younger, I believed that one day the world would be at peace and people would love each other. I'm not so sure about that now, but that doesn't mean we should give up trying.

Roller Skates

Peter Rognli

I once found a Canadian flag. It was discarded – crumpled up in the back room of the restaurant where I worked nights.

I took it.

Nobody would miss it. I lived in northern Minnesota, where American patriotism dripped with the sweat of a hard, working-class economy. And even close to the Canadian border, people didn't seem to put much stock in foreign national symbols. But all the same, a little tingle rush swept down the back of my spine – just enough to give me the chill of danger.

My adrenaline tolerance is set pretty low, so it doesn't take much to frighten or excite me. I remember at the roller rink when I was six, I'd gotten caught cheating on the Skee Ball game. The game was pretty simple. It was a cross between bowling, indoor bocce ball, and lawn darts. But instead of standing behind the line to throw at the target, I'd stand on the game, close to the target, and throw with an obvious advantage. It didn't take long before the roller-rink police – with her dark-frizzled hair and red roller rink sweatshirt – caught on to my version of the game.

"Come with me," she said in a tone that was meant to scare any average child. But I was not average; I was a good kid. I didn't sign up for this. I was here as a part of some field trip.

I would've rather been safely in my first grade classroom, filling out some worksheet on the color purple. But we all had to come roller skating.

The fluid in my spinal cord began to coagulate with fear as I lost feeling in the left side of my body. Roller skating was already too much of a rush for me—all those kids whizzing around like they were on...roller-skates. And carpeted walls.

The other kids flew fast turning around that track – like they were in a hot tub that suddenly broke – and so decided to make their own whirlpool by spinning, always spinning. While Paula Abdul ground into our fingertips on cassette from the booth with the fog machine and the big speakers and the black lights that lit up the guy's polyester shirt and yellow teeth. You know – the roller rink guy. The guy who wanted to be a DJ on the local pop radio a decade ago but decided to bide his time in the roller rink booth, as it's only two blocks from his mother's basement.

I could only skate in one direction: straight forward, which felt pretty good until I had to turn, and then smack, crash, carpet burn on the end of my nose. And that's how I knew roller skating. Staying close enough to the maroon carpet wall. Crashing on the floor when I wanted to get off the ride.

I'd go around the rink once or twice and then decide it was all too much for me and sit on the bench.

Except for this one time. I saw this kid playing a video game. Not your average violent game like Street Fighter or Mario Brothers, but Skee Ball. Now there was a wholesome game played by a family just dropping by the arcade after a picnic of tofu and whole wheat crackers. Just the right amount of adrenaline and excitement. And even better. There was a kid standing on the Skee Ball machine, throwing the wooden balls into the target.

So, I patiently waited my turn, and when the other kid was done, I stood on the Skee Ball machine, lobbing balls into the target. I was having a great time kicking Skee Ball butt when I had my encounter with the roller police, and was promptly dragged to the office.

It occurred to me then, and only then, that I had broken the rules. Those little machines spit out tickets. Tickets that could be exchanged for valuable prizes – like a pink bear, handcrafted in Indonesia by school children with tiny fingers. It occurred to me that bad kids would break the rules in order to get tickets in order to get a bear.

But I already had a bear. And currency had very little meaning to me. When my parents tried to give me my weekly allowance, I just stared at it and blinked. Money was like dried oregano – fun to crumple in your hands, but with very little value, except for a bit of seasoning.

I liked things with real value. Like my bear with the wind-up music box that played really, really slowly like Barry White calling out bingo numbers as the celebrity guest in some dank, church basement. Things that I liked had character, like my mom's canned choke cherry jelly that in December came out of the jar onto the bread in chunks that took a spatula to spread.

I liked things that carried their own experiences. Like my second year of college when I found that 1950s elementary school flip-top desk with the attached cracked wooded chair, painted in yellow lead, flaking off on the carpet. Inside, the desk was covered in crayon artwork from my parents' generation – baby boomers who, one decade later, would admonish traditions and promote a social revolution with cardboard signs, burnt bras, and puffy beards. A generation who, a decade later, would get married, have a baby, move from the suburbs, and start buying jelly from the grocery store.

I took the flag. To feel a little surge of adrenaline, and to have something in my pack-up-the-office box with character, I took the Canadian flag. Proud, I showed the flag to my roommate and best friend in the whole world, Ryan.

"Why do you have that?" he asked in a tone that was more snide than curious.

"So we can hang it on our deck."

We'd just gotten a place with a deck, and we were very proud of it. Actually, it was more of a balcony, made of rotten wood and about to fall down, but we liked the sound of calling it a deck. It made us feel domestic. "Hang it on the deck," I said, "so that way, the neighbors will ask, 'Who moved in next door?' and then they'll respond, 'I don't know. Some Canadians.'"

I thought this was hilarious. Ryan, however, found it marginally amusing, but tolerated the idea since I was his best friend in the whole world – and I'd said I was going to chip in for cable.

Ryan and I have been friends for what I'd like to say has been forever. But I remember meeting him in seventh grade, as we were both in Boy Scouts. Ryan was a cool-kid kid – with Doc Martins and pressed khaki pants that fit like they'd looked in the glossy picture of the catalog.

I wore dirty tennis shoes from Target with a purple bullseye painted on the heel. My pants fit like some washed-up glam rock star who'd taken one too many trips to the coke farm. The jeans that fit in September stretched tight against my hips by mid-October. The pants bottoms cut mid-way down my skinny calves like the Old Navy Capri pants that wouldn't come into style for another five years.

Under normal circumstances, I probably would never have met Ryan. But we had that one thing in common – Boy Scouts.

Boy Scouts. In junior high, being a Boy Scout was like being a communist during the middle of the 20th Century.

People ostracized me for my Target brand shoes. If anyone found out I was in Boy Scouts, they'd surely crucify me – my sad, deflated self-esteem lying there, bloody and limp, tacked up against some cool kid's locker like antlers from a hunting expedition. Being a Boy Scout was almost as bad as being gay.

Junior high kids talked about homosexuals as if they were a bunch of paranoid Puritans sitting around in a Boston coffee house discussing witches. Like the story of the Yeti that gets passed down generation to generation.

But even worse than some ominous monster with big teeth, sitting in the woods for decades waiting to pounce on the next innocent passerby – anybody could be gay. The witch could be that kid who wears the wrong baseball cap, or wears Target brand shoes with dirty capri pants. You could be the next fag – burned atop a bundle of flaming sticks.

Everybody worried about catching it. Gayness could be festering and breeding gay cancer cells in your gut, and you wouldn't even know it until one day you'd wake up with a limp wrist, an erection from some guy in your social studies class.

Boy Scouts were synonymous with queer. But Ryan was cool. Ryan was an openly Boy Scout cool kid – quite a big leap for junior high society. We always knew there were other Boy Scouts out there. They existed in band class, and at the corner lunch table that never quite filled up. But Boy Scouts would never talk to each other as Boy Scouts. We only talked under the guise of kids trying to fit in.

Ryan fit though. Somehow, when we all went through those awkward stages where our voices cracked and hair grew out of the left armpit but not the right, the cool kids maintained their charisma. Ryan was not shy about being a Boy Scout because that's what he did – because he was an honest and open guy.

Ryan learned to accept people. Or maybe he never forgot how to accept people. Or maybe he never developed a taste for a negative energy adrenaline rush. He never displayed someone's bloody self-esteem on the inside of his locker like the other cool kids. Ryan was my friend.

After high school, I went to a state university because the four-year institution was within the acceptable realm of expectations from my family and peer group.

After high school, Ryan went to a state community college because it was within the acceptable realm of expectations from his family and peer group.

He lived in Grand Rapids, and I lived in Bemidji – two northern Minnesota towns that are essentially the same thing: 14,000-person towns that serve as the economic base for the surrounding rural area. They both have a college, a small arts base, a Wal-Mart, and a struggling tourist-dependent (once natural resource-dependent) economy. And the culture of both towns promotes excessive alcohol consumption.

Grand Rapids and Bemidji are located just an hour away from one another on opposite sides of the Chippewa National Forest. After high school, Ryan and I made well-intentioned promises that we'd see each other as often as possible, as we were only an hour away. But "as much as possible" very quickly turns into "I can't get away this weekend." There's always a job to work or a paper to write or a fun party happening in my town. We didn't see each other very much. We called once in a while. I was usually stressed out for some stupid reason, and he was usually drunk for some stupid reason. We both had a difficult first couple of years of college, though I don't think either of us knew it at the time. Maybe it was because we felt pressure to be ultra-involved and active in everything. Maybe we felt the pressure to be the fun cool guy in our own respective towns, and tried our damnedest to live up to those expectations. Maybe the first couple years of anything are supposed to be tough – though we'd never want to admit it because a couple years is a long time, and why would I start anything if it was so damn hard?

In the end, we got through it. Neither of us dropped out of school, slit our wrists in the bathtub, or got thrown in jail. And our friendship survived. But the benefit of surviving came from the struggle.

Our sophomore year of school, I went to see my friend in Grand Rapids. I got into town on a Saturday evening in mid-February, and met him and his friends at the casino.

Casino is a loose term in northern Minnesota. Around a large metropolitan area, a casino is something that brings people in for a good time – the thrill they get from risking something of value. Then celebrating the adrenaline rush with a tasty fish fry, hopping back in their SUV, and driving back to the city and seventy thousand a year – happy to have lived on the edge for a while.

Casino in northern Minnesota is a place where people can come to sidetrack from real life, until the side track becomes the main track, and real life becomes a two-bedroom rambler in the woods where you never go hiking – with kids you never see, and 60 hours a week at the paper mill so you can blow a quarter of it every Saturday night here.

At the casino, I plopped a couple quarters into the spiny, blinky machines, lost both times, and walked around in search of the pop cart. On my quest for free pop, I spent five dollars on a soft pack of Marlboro Lights – because slowly poisoning myself with over-priced, charred toxic chemicals, proven to kill me over time, is more exciting than gambling.

I lit up, and took a deep, contemplative drag.

Whenever I don't feel sure of my stance, my body, my clothes, or if everyone is looking at the zit on my forehead that I just tried to pop in the bathroom but got blood on the mirror instead, smoking makes me feel comfortable – like a soft little squid squirting a cloud of ink to cover up the fact that it has eight legs.

From inside a puff of smoke, I'd drop off the world's radar. I'd stare like a camo-covered hunter in a duck blind standing knee-deep in swamp. I decided that the most interesting part of the casino was the people mesmerized by the flashing lights and the blinking sounds. I marveled at how pathetic it was – laying fifty-dollar bills on a felt green table for a stupid card game. In reality, I was too scared to even play.

After the casino got old, we all went to a late night party in a cabin in the woods – where someone pegged me as gay. It was the leader of the pack – the big one with the protruding underbite, bad teeth, and round Kodiak tin growing like a tumor from his ass – we'll call him Erg.

Erg had gotten jealous because I was talking to some ex-girlfriend of his. So he decided to pick on the fact that I looked and acted a bit queer when compared to the rest of the flannel-wearing crowd. In a small cabin, in the big woods, Erg was forming a gang of his angry friends.

I, of course, was oblivious to anything that was happening. I was drunk.

The world has happy drunks and unhappy drunks. I am a happy drunk – one who reverts to the bubbling, giggly little kid playing toy cars on the brown linoleum floor, making vroom-vroom noises between flapping lips. I sat on the couch with the girl I wasn't supposed to be talking to – gabbing away in slurred speech.

Ryan, however, always the concerned friend, was attempting to diffuse the situation, by making peace with the Erganites.

Erg was drunk and angry, and I suspect he was always angry. Alcohol brings out the real person deep down insides – the person that existed before roller rinks or capri pants – the child. Erg's child was insecure, mean, and had breath that smelled of Doritos, Kodiak mint, and Keystone Light.

Before I knew what was happening, Ryan's friends were coming up to me and telling me they had my back. I blinked confused, but Ryan took me aside and explained that there was a giant man with friends in the corner who wanted to kick my ass for acting too queer, but it was okay because they had my back.

Not wanting to be the catalyst for some violent confrontation, I decided, in my childhood drunken mind, that if I could just talk to the Erg creature – if I could just explain to him that sexuality really isn't that big of a deal, and we should just accept people for who they are – I could diffuse the whole situation. Erg would realize that his homophobia was the result of something his father said after coming home with one too many Lord Calvert n' Cokes from the local VFW. The whole gang would politely apologize, tip their hats goodnight, and call their friends for a sober ride home.

But it didn't work that way. Through his yellow teeth, Erg yelled something about Jesus and faggots and hell; I yelled something about Jesus and how he could go to hell and the marvelous taste of salt.

Minutes later, a fight broke out while I stood hunkered in the corner. It lasted only a few seconds. Erg's friends punched Ryan's friends; Ryan's friends punched Erg's friends; someone got a bloody nose; and the Erg crowd scattered – hopping in their trucks, and speeding back to town.

The fight looked awkward, like sheep trying to dance on their back two legs. Secretly, I'd hoped for something cool out of that action movie where that guy got spun around and then thrown across the table. But the human body has no beauty in anger. It just looked stupid – like a kid learning to roller skate.

There was nothing neat, nothing cool, but nothing terribly tragic or dramatic either. After the Ergs ran away, everyone that was left high-fived, lamented about how tough they were, and shot a game of pool. I lit a cigarette, tried to exhale, but the smoke from my lungs did nothing to hide how conspicuous I felt. I sat on the couch feeling exposed, as if my toupee had fallen into the tomato soup during an awkward first date.

But in the end, no one really cared. Except for the awkward guy in the Metallica shirt that came over to hit on me, no one stopped for a second to turn around and see the queer in the corner. No one even stopped playing pool. And I was left sitting there – reclined on the couch – shoulders hunched, puffing hard, and ignoring the pudgy guy batting his eyes and saying, "I'm not gay – but . . ."

Listen

Jamie Nelson

A good friend of mine from North Carolina once asked why I was o upset after my girlfriend broke up with me. "After all," she said, it couldn't possibly be worse than if a real guy broke up with you."

I told her to imagine her dream guy breaking up with her. Then nultiply the pain by ten. See, because my girlfriend was real, and ince she was of the gender that actually steals my heart, it hurt even vorse. And she still had my favorite damn pair of shoes.

Although I grew up traveling with the carnival—living with les-ians, blacks, Hispanics, tall gay men with short legs, bearded ladies vho dated the fat ladies who sang—it never occurred to me that might be gay. I knew I liked one thing: pizza. And, from what I nderstood, pizza was more likely to make you fat than pregnant. ame with lesbianism.

The gay thing might not be so shocking, but here's the shocker: I vent to college, and was in a sorority with *straight* girls. (By the way, here is no such thing.) So, one of my straight sorority sisters and I vere discussing our lesson in Women's Studies, and the inevitable appened:

"Have you ever?"

"Nope."

"You?"

"Nope."

"Wanna?"

"Okay."

But we didn't, because she tried it with another one of my straight sorority sisters, and that killed it for me. But, it also piqued my interest about why I couldn't stop dreaming about it.

So, one day after class, I asked my lesbian professor if she thought I were gay. She looked me up and down—my long hair, my sorority sweatshirt, my boyfriend's fraternity lavalier around my neck—and she said, in her Sylvester Stallone, locker-room-like lesbian drawl, yet with a Southern accent, "No."

After being engaged about five or six or whatever times, then breaking up with the guys, I decided to make a change: The next guy I almost marry will have to agree that I can have all the women I want. Perfect! Now, if I could only find the women. (The guy part of the equation was easier than finding lint on your shirt in a bar with a black light.)

So, I swore off all men. Met a gorgeous model. She had a boyfriend. I never let on that I wanted to bury my nose behind her soft sweet, earlobe. In fact, I had never actually been with a woman. I was twenty-five.

And just as the bear went over the mountain, you know what happened next. And, *oh, my God, did it happen*!

And you're wondering what happened to her boyfriend. Yeah, I don't care, either.

So, I called my mom the next morning and told her the great news.

"Mooom! I finally figured it out. I'm GAY! Woo-hooo! And, ya know, it doesn't taste that ba-…Mom?"

So, she called me back about a half-hour later to tell me that she just spoke with her friend Michael. Michael said that he knew he was gay when he was thirteen, so if I didn't know by then, great news—it's just a phase. Oy. Apparently it's Okay for everyone *else's* kid to be gay.

My mom took a year or so to cool off—which is better than one of my straight sorority sisters who told me she had a religious problem with me, so we couldn't be friends anymore. Better than the friend who kicked me out of her wedding party.

Fast forward six years later: I decided against marrying a guy who would let me have all the women I want. I don't want all the women. I just want the one perfect woman to whom I am now happily engaged. And Sheryl Crow.

My ex-girlfriend can keep that damn pair of shoes she never returned, and *no,* they were *not* Birkenstocks!

My mom has now become a support for other parents of fabulous gay children.

My friend with the religious problem has since married the wrong guy, divorced, and moved to New York City where she and I are the best of friends again. I always appreciated her honesty, communication, and space she needed to grow.

The one who kicked me out of her wedding now has a child. I pray to the good Lord that her child grows up to be a strong, healthy, community-active butch-dyke!

Sweet Home

Angelique Chambers

The boy on the couch is trying not to look at us. He's trying really hard. I can tell he's only half-listening to what his mother is reading to him out of the prospective student guide brochure to SUNY Oswego. She keeps jabbing the page for emphasis, no doubt hyped up on complimentary coffee, but what he's really interested in is us: a faggot, two butch dykes, and a femme.

All around us, high school seniors and their parents wander through the maze of informational booths set up in the student union, eager to learn all that Oswego has to offer. We watch as they visit the honors program table, intramurals, Residence Life and Housing, Black Student Union, History Club. There is a small crowd gathering in front of the Juggling Club table watching a short girl with curly hair turn three tennis balls into a continuous yellow blur.

"Maybe if somebody could juggle, we'd get more visitors," Sarah suggests, and we all laugh.

We don't really expect many people to approach our table. Mostly we're just here to let prospective students know we exist. At any rate, our table's hard to miss. We've got a Pride Flag laid out on the table and it's covered with books and magazines from our library. A purple bandana that boasts "Gay R Us" hangs from the white poster board sign labeled Rainbow Alliance. I'm wearing embroidered jeans and my "I prefer womyn" t-shirt, and I'm handing out flyers to people who are, for the most part, desperately trying to avoid our table. A good number of the people who have sat on the couches nearest to us have stared, but somehow I think this boy is different. He doesn't look disgusted; he looks curious and scared in a way that I think I understand. I wonder if maybe next fall he'll stop by our table at the student involvement fair when his mom won't be around to question his motives. Maybe he'll take a flyer and a sticker and ask about our meetings. And then maybe he will actually show up. Or maybe I'll never see this kid again. But, just in case, I flash him a smile.

I don't remember if anyone from Rainbow Alliance smiled at me when I first visited SUNY Oswego five years ago, and I don't remember visiting the table. I was eighteen and already engaged to a boy four years older than me, living in the tiny town of Lafayette, New York, where I grew up. I was positive I was going to get my bachelor's degree and leave Oswego in no more than four years. I was positive that sleeping with Teisha in high school didn't really matter much. I was positive that my intense attraction to girls my whole life was surpassed by my dedication to Jason. I was positive I was going to marry him.

*

Sarah and I fight every time I cut her hair; tonight is no exception. The electric clippers hum against the palm of my hand as I run them in a line that I hope is straight across her head. We bought these almost a year ago. Sarah's hair was getting too long and we knew we couldn't afford to go to Esther, the college beautician. Esther who cuts only with a straight razor. Esther who asks over and over how we met and tells us about her no good Dominican boyfriends over loud Latin music. She's the best, but she's expensive, and Sarah says she never cuts it short enough. Hair cutters in town are out of the question. In this town, Sarah gets called "sir" more often than not, but somehow hairdressers always know. They look at Sarah in her men's department button-down shirts, black jeans, army boots and still they see a girl. We bring a picture of Sarah with her best men's haircut, spiked and gelled to perfection. It doesn't matter. They add mousse, fluff, and Sarah ends up embarrassed and paying money to wear a hat home. We've never tried a barber. I doubt it would be pretty.

I cut it short enough, but I don't believe that I'll ever stop worrying that the lines are crooked. Somehow, I think that a perfect haircut offers protection. I want people passing her on the street to think "What a great haircut" instead of "Fuckin' queer." I know a little ego goes a long way for butches, and I know it's all I can offer when she's out there on the street. I feel like I can never get it just right, never good enough, never perfect. I see the slightest jagged edge where there should be an even line, and I know I cannot offer armor to the outside world. I know this haircut won't protect her. I begin to cry, and when she asks what's wrong, I can't tell her, so I yell. I say, "I never wanted to cut your fucking hair. I hate when you make me do this," and she says, "Don't worry, I won't ask you to do anything for me ever again." Eventually we shut up or cry, or both, until the clippers go back into the medicine cabinet for another month.

I decide that it's done. I rub my fingers over her scalp and feel the hair bristling against my hand. It's too short to grab right now but it grows back fast. In just a few days, I'll be just able to grasp it by the roots and tip her head back for a kiss. I brush the stray hair off the back of her neck and hand her a mirror.

Sarah looks down at the thick mat of hair at her feet, runs both hands over her head and grins.

*

One of the advantages to being femme in a small town is nobody suspects that you're queer. When I walk alone, nobody yells "dyke" or throws garbage at me, ever present events in the lives of Sarah and our butch friends. Most people don't see past my earrings or lip gloss and see a lesbian. The kids at this group home are no exception. So far, my sexuality has been on a don't ask, don't tell basis. "It's like the military," I joke to my friends in Rainbow Alliance, the LGBT group that I run on campus. Still, sometimes I feel as if I'm living a double life.

I know these kids, raised in Oswego County, will not react with anything less than animosity to my queerness. I tell myself that I am here to earn internship credit and gain experience working with youth, not come out. I tell myself my sexuality has nothing to do with my job here. Secretly, I don't want their first experience with a gay person to be someone who doles out consequences for unfinished chores. So I'm surprised and somewhat unnerved when Emily grabs my left hand and inspects the class ring I'm wearing on my middle finger.

"Whose ring is this?" she asks.

Before I can conjure up an answer, Anna replies, "It probably belongs to her boyfriend, retard."

"Uh-uh. It says Sarah on it," Emily says looking triumphant.

They both turn to stare at me. I'm not sure what they expect me to say. Fear sits heavily in my stomach. Suddenly, I feel like I've never come out to anyone before. Saying the words partner or girlfriend seems like an insurmountable feat. I feel my face growing hot.

"It belongs to someone who means a lot to me."

This is not the answer they want to hear. They turn away, annoyed at my vagueness, or lack of entertainment, or perhaps at something else all together. At 15, there's a lot at which to be pissed.

Hours later, the ring presses into my thigh through the pocket of my jeans as I'm in the office writing in the logbooks. I want to get through the mountain of paperwork before me and get home to Sarah, but the girls keep calling to me from their bedroom.

"Angel, come in here, we gotta ask you a question."

"You gotta go to sleep," I reply, but I'm already up and across the hall standing in their doorway.

"Hey, um, do you have a boyfriend?"

I sigh. "No, now go to sleep. Please."

"Wait, one more question."

"What?" I already know what they are going to ask. These kids are smarter than I give them credit for.

"You ever had a girlfriend?"

I try to mask the feeling of tightness in my throat and chest. "Go to sleep," I say and head back to the office, trying to ignore the giggling behind my back.

*

When people want to ride with us to the nearest gay club, we tell them to bring a coat. Our hand-me-down Chevy Cavalier lacks the luxuries of heat and turn signals—but it has new tires and fits five so most people don't mind. Tonight we head toward Syracuse at 75 miles per hour, shivering and singing along to the radio. We get there in under 40 minutes, a new record.

We show our IDs at the door and pay the three dollar cover charge. It is Thursday, college night, and the bar is swarming with students and drag queens. The show won't start for about half an hour, and the queens are cruising the crowd, making small talk over the dance music, ensuring tips from their fans when they perform.

Everyone is excited. Charades Nightclub and Showbar has been closed for remodeling and most of us haven't seen each other in over a month. This evening's hostess, Frita Lay, saunters up to us, smiling. After a round of hugs, she asks if we've been going anywhere else for the past few weeks.

"Nope," replies Sarah, "Nowhere else to go, Frita. We missed this place."

"What, no queer bars in Oswego?" she asks in mock surprise.

*

Debbie leans over the green felt, adjusts her stick, squints and sinks the eight ball.

"Nice shot." Sarah digs quarters out of her pocket for another game.

We're at Toucans Tropical Bar, a local bar that caters to the college students in Oswego. We've stopped trying to go to the bars frequented by "townies," unnerved by the stares we get. We're grateful there has never been a problem here. The bartenders are mostly college students who don't do double takes when Sarah hands over a driver's license clearly marked female. They have a jukebox and two pool tables, and as long as we don't show up on Saturday, it isn't crowded.

Tonight, we have one of the pool tables in the back room to ourselves. Debbie and Sarah share pitchers of cheap beer and try to out-butch each other by deliberately calling tough shots. Garth Brooks blares through the speakers. The three of us sing along at the top of our lungs, and I know "Sweet Home Alabama" is coming up next. Full of alcohol and laughter, we aren't paying attention to anyone else in the bar, including the guys playing at the table a few feet away.

I don't know when they started staring, but when I look up, I stop laughing. Angry eyes above a pool stick aimed right at us. Sarah's clenched jaw tells me that she's well aware of being watched; still she tries to play it cool, throws back the rest of her beer, bends over the pool table and misses an easy shot. This time Debbie doesn't tease her. The guys are talking now, but I can't hear what they're saying. I know this is the last game Debbie and Sarah will be playing though quarters are lined up neatly on the polished wood of the table and it's only eleven. They're down to just the 8 ball anyway.

"Fuckin' dykes," one of the guys mutters, and I hop off my stool.

Sarah leans over Debbie's shoulder, "Come on, time ta go."

The bartender waves and smiles at us as we walk out. Walking down Water Street, the air is cold, Sarah's arm is around my shoulder, and I can still hear the jukebox playing "Lord, I'll be coming home to you." Quarters jingle in my pocket. We left the 8 ball on the table.

*

It's strange, feeling like an elder at twenty-three, but here I am sitting in the Rainbow Alliance office almost a year after my own graduation feeling old. Not old in a bad way like how my mother and co-workers groan over gray hairs and aching backs, but old in the way grandmothers must feel when they tell their grandchildren what the world was like when they grew up. Old like somebody who has helped build something and then watched it change.

Sarah and I are telling a story we've told a thousand times. We're telling Aaron and Jes how we met, our coming out. We pepper this story with little historical facts about the Rainbow Alliance.

"Oh, remember the big gay parties freshman year?" Sarah asks me.

I turn to Aaron. "The leaders of Rainbow all used to live in this big, dirty house on 5th Avenue. A couple times each semester, they'd throw a keg party and everyone, even faculty, showed up. They'd buy really cheap beer and tell everyone it was Bud. And when you opened the fridge, there'd be nothing but JELL-O shots all lined up on trays like Pride Flags."

I don't know who lives in that house now, with its ten-foot plywood dining table and drafty windows, and it doesn't matter. This reminiscence isn't about how many queer people will pay five dollars to drink cheap beer out of plastic cups, or which professors ate too much gelatin spiked with cheap vodka. It's about people kissing and not looking over their shoulders. What we're telling Jes and Aaron is this: Family is important. Being queer in Oswego, this strange place where college students and factory workers and tourists all walk the same sidewalks, has taught me a lot about family.

Sometimes I wonder if we will always be happy here, spending time in the Rainbow Alliance office organizing events and telling stories. Most of our friends are students who will leave just days after getting their diploma or professors who are constantly applying to other places, tired of this white bread Republican town. I wonder if, in twenty years, I will still feel like an elder in this family of queers, or if I'll begin to feel like an old woman playing chaperone at the senior prom.

Maureen tells me of the queer community in another place hundreds of miles away. She says she misses Tulsa, where she came out, and I wonder if our hearts are always set in the place where we first told ourselves the truth about who we are. In Oswego, three and half years ago, I first called myself a dyke. Maybe those words transformed this place, in my heart, into my home. Maybe in that moment I became, like a tree rooted in the earth of this place.

Last week at our annual Rainbow Alliance Ally Banquet, Melissa called Sarah and me her queer parents and nobody laughed. Her "real" family lives in Long Island. Her "real" family pretends she isn't queer. Her "real" family tells her, "Act straight or you can't see your seven-year-old brother." When she said to seventy other people that we were family, I looked around the room and saw people clapping, smiling and nodding their heads.

*

The hot air in my face makes me dizzy as I rush out of the air-conditioned cave of Real Deals dollar store. I'm ten minutes late clocking out. Tourists have flooded Oswego for the annual Harborfest, bringing with them whiny kids, expensive boats, and a grand appreciation for alcohol. This afternoon the dollar store is crowded as they search for cheap plastic cups and toys for their kids that can be thrown away or abandoned in their hotel rooms when they pack up and head home.

Sarah waits for me, leaning against the ice machine. Her face is shiny and pink from spending too much time in the sun. She's carrying a bulging plastic grocery bag.

"I spent the whole day on campus with Debbie," she says, "away from the tourists. We found a pear tree."

"Where?"

"Down by the lake, behind the health center." She holds out the bag for me to see. It is filled with small green pears.

I smile. Leave it to them to find adventure. I reach in and take a pear. It is crisp and sweet when I bite into it; the fruit is grainy on my tongue.

"Good, huh?" Sarah asks. I nod, still chewing. "The thing is," she continues, "the best pears, the really good ones, are at the top of the tree."

"Okay," I reply, knowing this is heading somewhere.

"Debbie and I thought you could climb it and throw them down to us. What do ya think? Good day for climbing trees. Lots of sun."

I look down at my sandals, clearly built more for style than durability or athletic function. For a moment, I ponder my other shoes—black heels, lace-up platform boots, wedge-heeled sneakers—and wonder if I own any footwear suitable for climbing trees. I start laughing.

"Aren't you butches supposed to have spent your childhood climbing trees and playing in the mud? You two must have experience. You do it."

"You're smaller. We could boost you up. Think of it, all that fresh fruit completely free."

And suddenly I can see myself, barefoot, climbing despite my short summer skirt. The sun shining in my eyes, the sound of waves crashing on the rocks, two pairs of hands below me ready to steady me, one of my hands on the rough bark of the pear tree and the other reaching up, almost touching the ripest piece of fruit.

My Familiar

Charity Warren

"Quit walkin' life that!"

"You look like a damn football player."

"Folks gonna think you're one of them feminists, missy. Or some bull dyke."

"Same difference, mmm-hmmm."

As the door to the convenience store shut behind me, I turned to find a group of hard-looking old men playing cards next to the window, drinking sodas and smoking cigarettes at a table wedged between a stack of motor oil and several cases of Lone Star beer. They all looked ancient to me, each well past fifty, and they were all staring at me. Smoke from their cigarettes mingled with sun rays and dust specks, casting a tobacco-fumed shroud around their lean, lined faces.

Nervous, I glanced around the aisles, hoping fervently they were looking at someone else, but finding no other likely suspect. The counter clerk, a plump, matronly woman in her late fifties who smelled of donuts and laundry detergent, eyed me with an expression of both amusement and reproach. A creepy sensation of "otherness" settled onto my shoulders, making me shrug involuntarily. I had been singled out, targeted, culled from the herd for some weakness or infirmity. To a twelve-year-old, this was the Kiss of Death. Dully, as though watching from a distance, I felt a one-word question pass over my lips: "What?"

The man in the red flannel shirt answered, waving his cigarette pointedly at me. "I said young ladies shouldn't walk like football players. It ain't proper. You look a damn fool." This was greeted with nods of approval from the other two men, who looked at me severely as though I'd been filching pies from the windowsill.

With a stab of defensiveness and an impressive lack of forethought, I shot back, "What's wrong with how I walk?" Comments on my walk touched a nerve with me, as my parents couldn't afford the corrective shoes I had needed as a child for a foot that turned in slightly. Pumped by emotions and adrenaline, I added indignantly, "And what if I want to be a football player?!"

Red Flannel and John Deere Cap laughed delightedly at this, but Blue Flannel, a hard-looking man in his late seventies, coughed on his soda, spluttering Coca-Cola onto the table. "Don't you be smart to your elders, girlie. Girls don't play football, everyone knows that. Girls can be cheerleaders or help the Booster club. But they don't play football, and that's all she wrote. And don't act like you didn't strut in here swinging your shoulders and carrying yourself like a man."

Partly out of insecure frustration (I did NOT strut) and partly from a deep-seated talent for antagonizing anyone in my vicinity, I popped off, "Well, how am I supposed to walk? Keep my head down and walk into doors? Or should I just stand around and wait for some guy to come along and open it for me? And," I added in a pique of righteous pre-teen rebellion, "what if I am a feminist? Or ...that other thing you said?" The matronly clerk behind me "tsked" loudly, and I felt embarrassment heating my cheeks. Silence fell. The men stared at me mouths agape in disbelief, sodas and cigarettes forgotten halfway to lips. Oops.

What erupted was largely an unintelligible outpouring of oaths, sputters and righteous indignation that I thankfully couldn't quite make out. I heard something about needing a good old-fashioned switching interspersed with severe comments about my mother's good sense (or lack thereof), but the switching part was enough for me. Faced with such an onslaught, I did what any self-respecting twelve-year-old would do. I fled. Abandoning all dignity and ignoring angry mutters of, "Come back here! I'm not done talking to you," I turned heel and ran out the door, through the parking lot and over the neighboring railroad tracks, where I finally slowed to a furtive walk and tried my best to look perfectly normal.

Welcome to Crowley, Texas, 1986.

*

Several years ago, while still an undergraduate at Texas Christian University, I read an essay written by Sigmund Freud, whom most remember as the psychologist with the cigar complex and Oedipus fixation. For this article, entitled "The Uncanny," Freud ventured briefly into the world of literary criticism and explored fear of the "uncanny" or, in German, *unheimlich.* Though I initially found it difficult reading, Freud had a fascinating and compelling point: The things most frightening to us are the things which are most familiar, yet altered in a way as to be unfamiliar. Deep in the recesses of the darkest closets, haunting the corners of the imagination, we do not find things utterly alien and incomprehensible. Instead, we find the things well-known to us, revealed as something different while remaining the same.

When I reflect back on that day in the convenience store, I wonder what frightened or disturbed a group of men so much that they felt the need to harass and embarrass a twelve-year-old girl. I doubt they would agree that they were frightened at all. They were just correcting a wayward youth and teaching her wholesome values, a prime example of the village raising the child. Yet it seems clear to me that there was an underlying anxiety, something gnawing at them from some place deep within, to justify the vehemence of their attacks. Accusing a local girl on the cusp of adulthood of being a bull dyke? No fear there.

And what of my own fear? Why did I turn and run, trying to blend in with the scenery rather than confide in my mother, a friend, anyone, what had happened? In truth, telling someone would have acknowledged that those old men struck dangerously close to home. I know this now. At the time, however, I was twelve, scared and deeply ashamed for reasons unknown. I didn't need to dig any deeper than that. I didn't want to dig any deeper than that. Excavation would have uncovered an equivocal dilemma I was not prepared to face. So I ran and concealed my fears, not understanding I was also concealing the fears of three old men at a table in a convenience store in Crowley, Texas, 1986. Mine, theirs. Same difference.

It seems paradoxical in some ways that I felt compelled to remain secreted, closeted, about my sexual orientation. After all, romantic idealizations of small-town life describe a world of acceptance, of loving, warm people that invite strangers to dinner. Everyone knows everyone else, and no one has any real secrets. Yet one of the peculiar realities of growing up a closet gay in a small town is a kind of social schizophrenia, an odd juxtaposition of "traditional" values against a sometimes brutal, pulsating fear of the Other. Instead of *Leave it to Beaver* I found myself starring in a bizarre Norman Rockwellian version of *Deliverance.* For twenty-seven years, I traversed a surreal landscape of wholesome values, hardworking citizens and a strong church going community of intolerant rednecks who parked on the front lawn, their '57 Chevys, equipped with gun racks. Homosexuality didn't exist, at least not in any tangible way. Gays existed the same way that Satanic cults stealing and sacrificing local children existed, on the fringes of the imagination, a bogeyman or a scapegoat. In polite society, they simply weren't discussed, or if they were, it was in the form of derisive jokes or political slander.

*

The matronly woman at the convenience store counter in Crowley, Texas, 1986, leans over and whispers to Red Flannel, "I hear Sara Jenkins is running for school board, can you believe it? She's a single mother, mmm-hmmm. Probably one of them feminists. They're all lezbeeyuns, you know, feminists. I learned all about it on PBS last night."

*

Yet homosexuality did exist. It existed in the jokes, the slander, the silence. The very means used to suppress it made it real, confirmed its existence. It existed in me. I never told anyone, terrified of even admitting it to myself, for I, too, was afraid of the Other. In very real ways, I was exactly what Crowley, Texas, 1986, feared. I was the Other, but I was hidden within the mundane and open banality of small-town life. I went to their schools, received good grades, babysat their children, danced in their streets at county fairs and played my music entirely too loud. I was fundamentally the same as any other kid my age in Crowley, a pain in the neck, but more or less normal.

Yet a defining, central part of me was trapped in a closet that just happened to be in their house. Why, then, did I not let anyone know I was there? We stood on opposite sides of the same door, each afraid to open up and see what lay beyond. Each of us existed in the same space in two separate worlds. Mine, theirs. Same difference.

When friends and family ask me why it took almost thirty years for me to come out, I usually give a canned response of, "I didn't want to be beaten with sticks." Certainly I was afraid of revealing myself, yet fear never came from a distinct, definable source. I never quaked with terror at the image of Bubba running me over with his '78 Ford pickup or getting beaten up by school thugs. Such things were a real possibility that frightened me, but mangled flesh has nothing on a tortured soul (and teenagers have particularly tortured souls, as any parent will confirm). Fear of rejection, particularly from my mother, who frequently used homophobic epithets to vent against her "lezbo" boss, scared me, yet not enough to keep me closeted.

After much introspection and self-confrontation, I find that the same fear that both repressed and confirmed homosexuality in Crowley was the same fear that motivated me to be silent. What terrified me the most, what led me to pretend to be straight, to date males, even to marry one, was the very same universal small town fear that led three old men to harangue a twelve-year-old girl: fear of what's already there, hidden in plain view. Concealed, yet revealed. Same difference. Subtle indoctrination works, hate crimes need not apply.

By the time I was old enough to understand the nature of homosexuality, I had been sufficiently indoctrinated to reject it as vile, unnatural, and ungodly. No one ever sat me down and preached to me about the horrific sins committed by homosexuals; there was no need. The slander, jokes and derision that were a part of everyday life served the dual purpose confirming that gays existed and educating me about their sinful lives. They didn't know they were joking about me. The moral vanguard of Crowley, Texas, didn't realize that I, personally, played a starring role in the joke about the lesbian, the nun and the chimp who walked into a bar. Unknowingly, Crowley, Texas, held a mirror in front of me bearing the words, "Caution: Objects in Mirror Are More Evil Than They Appear."

I recognized myself in the put-downs. I saw myself reflected in their jokes, but the reflections sickened me, frightened me, left me praying to wake up as someone else. Someone real. Someone of Truth. I lived in a carnival house of mirrors, seeing only twisted, perverse deviations of me, living through the eyes of everyone else. I lived in fear of transforming into a hideous wretch of a creature, of going from a blonde-haired, blue-eyed country girl to a black-studded-leather-adorned gargoyle with a crew cut and a ticket straight to the gates of Hell. I feared what Freud considered among the scariest of all things: the familiar becoming the unfamiliar. I feared exactly the same thing a group of old men sitting at a table in a convenience store feared in Crowley, Texas, 1986.

*

A group of giggling girls scuttle past me as I open my locker in the hallways of Crowley High, 1990. I hear the word "dyke" and an outburst of shrieking laughter. My pulse quickens, and I cast a furtive glance over my shoulder. The new girl stands off to the side, by herself as usual. She's dressed all in black and seems engrossed in a copy of Kurt Vonnegut's *Slaughterhouse Five*, but I know better. I see the tears welling. She heard. I check my lipstick and hair in my locker mirror, doing my best to look perfectly normal. It was the Other girl. Not me. They weren't talking about me.

*

Same difference.

Ovaltine Dreams
Growing Up Gay in Villa Park, Illinois
Kenneth Pobo

For many years, I thought there was just one Villa Park—mine—only to learn in high school that California had one, too. I figured theirs smelled of oranges and grapefruits, but the California Villa Park probably did not have what we had—the Ovaltine factory, a square brick structure that covered a block, had its own water tower, and blared a shrill whistle each workday at noon. We walked in a smell of burnt chocolate. I didn't hate drinking Ovaltine, and sometimes my parents and I would watch TV and drink it. But Dad preferred Budweiser; Mom, Diet Rite Cola; and I liked Coke.

Our street, Villa Avenue, felt secure. When the neighborhood kids were young, moms kept house. Back doors stayed open. My mom couldn't, and still can't, drive. No problem. Our next door neighbor, Marge, could and would be right there in an emergency. If we needed food or household items, we could walk to the business district, only four blocks up. There, we had two pharmacies, a hobby shop, a Ben Franklin's dime store, a bank, and a dress shop. A Pay Less grocery store and the post office were a couple more blocks.

An only child, I didn't feel lonely because there were kids my age on both sides of our house. John Stendo lived to our left, John Baxter to our right—friends and playmates throughout my years in Villa Park. We invented games and biked as often as we could, our territory expanding as we grew. When I was alone in my room, I wasn't sad. I had a family of stuffed animals, some of which are still with me today. Hector, a brown stuffed dog that my dad had won for my mom at a carnival when they were dating, guarded the foot of my bed. I called Hector my wife. Hector still guards the same spot even though I'm a thousand miles away now in Pennsylvania. Harry the stuffed terrier is my kitchen god, watching me now just as he did in fifth grade.

My dad's parents lived in Elmhurst, one town east, and my other grandparents lived in Lombard, one town west. Elmhurst at the time was the biggest town in DuPage County. Each Saturday, my parents would drop me off at my grandparents'. My grandmother and I would play canasta and my grandfather would sometimes drive me to downtown Elmhurst. When I became a teenager, he'd take me to the Elmhurst Music-Mart and slip me money. Lombard was smaller, more like Villa Park, only with a little more traffic and better quality stores.

Once I got old enough to bike longer distances, the two Johns and I would ride to E.J. Korvette's, a big store in Elmhurst. I got my first 45s there. Oh, that thrilling day when I held "Hanky Panky" by Tommy James and the Shondells in my hand, forty-nine cents. My allowance, two quarters for spending, a quarter for my piggy bank, and a quarter for church, didn't allow for big spending. Candy, popsicles, records, and presents for relatives ate it up.

Getting to "the city," meaning Chicago, took a half hour train ride. I didn't take the train alone until high school. Some members of my family and neighbors told me about the terrible trouble that could happen to me there. I could be robbed or killed. Many in the suburbs felt they had "escaped" the city. They really meant they could be racists and few would call them on it. Also, cities got dirty but suburbs stayed clean—mowing the lawn, almost a religious act. They really meant people who were different from them live in cities and should stay there. We did not want to be infected.

I don't know if I got wrapped in a blue blanket after I was born. My parents debated whether to name me Kenneth, Steven, or Eric if I were a boy; I would have been Nancy had I been a girl. There was no book of names for a gay baby. Kenneth had to do.

To people on Villa Avenue, it was not conceivable in 1954 that parents such as mine could have a baby who would turn out gay. Had I been born with a defect like a cleft palate, my parents would have received ample sympathy and help. If these same sympathetic and helpful people had a way to see into the future that Kenny would be gay, the sympathy would have staled, the help gone rotten. Back then, and sadly in much of the world today, to be gay is seen as defective, sub-human. I wasn't defective.

Nobody had the magic TV set that George Burns had on *The Burns and Allen Show.* George could keep an eye on Gracie and the kooky plot developments in the privacy of his upstairs office. No one (except Jack Benny) had any clue about this set. I'm lucky the adults had no set. I grew up under the hot breath of neighborhood and religious expectations. I looked normal. In photographs, I'm a smiling, auburn-haired baby. As I grew, I looked thin, and in summer, my crew cut hair turned blond. I'm glad my parents had no TV that could watch my every move. I felt watched enough.

Some of my early behaviors suggested gay stereotypes. I loved playing dress-up and paper dolls. I didn't need anyone other than my stuffed animal menagerie to enjoy those games. Dressing up let me be a star, someone beautiful and famous. I'd wrap my blankets and sheets around me, thinking I had my own TV show. Jackie, who lived two houses behind us until I was six, was my favorite dress-up partner. Slender and blond, she could smuggle things from her sister Eve's closet. Her brother Carl joined us once, but got bored quickly and ran off. I missed her when they moved. The neighborhood boys wanted to play with toy trucks (boring!); to play army (a lot of running around and shooting at each other with plastic guns our parents got us at Ben Franklin's); or to play whiffle ball, baseball, and basketball. Whiffle ball I enjoyed, even though I wasn't good at it. Sometimes I played baseball and basketball too, not wanting to be left out.

My interest in playing dress-up did not go unnoticed. When John Stendo and I got into a ridiculous fight, as kids do, our dads got involved. His dad came banging on our back screen door, yelling, and my dad responded in kind. His dad called me a "sissy." I knew this was a bad thing to be. I didn't know why, but it was one of those moments where, dimly, a light started to flicker on. I was different from his son.

Dress-up didn't last beyond early elementary school, though I clung to my stuffed animals into junior high. Today, I have little interest in doing drag, though I admire drag queens for their style and courage. How sad that many gays, in order to get the rights we are routinely denied, feel we must look straight, be "straight-acting" (awful phrase!), and imitate straight people. The drag queens rang our chimes of freedom at the Stonewall Bar in 1969. The assimilators mostly headed for the hills.

In grade school, I preferred the company of girls. Boys meant sports, and sports meant competition. Girls had fun games like Chinese jump rope. Girls, mostly, were nicer than boys—at least to me. The bullies who didn't like me were always boys. They smelled my difference. Going to school often made me scared and nervous, but I was afraid to tell anyone. I was learning that boys hold things in. We start storing up our heart attacks in childhood so they can bloom in our forties and fifties.

My parents believe deeply in education. My mother finished high school and went to work after graduation until she married my dad in 1952. My dad went to Elmhurst College as a science major. Like me when I went to college, he, too, lived at home rather than in a dorm. I used to think it didn't seem possible that I was his son. I now see some similarity. He studied ways to map particles of light. I study ways to map syllables of words in a poem.

Education didn't get boxed up in school rooms. Every year, we went to northern Wisconsin; they wanted me to enjoy nature, which I did, and still do. We rented a cabin on Little Lake St. Germain. I couldn't swim, but I plotched in the water, built sand castles, even went fishing in a rowboat with my dad. I could manage an hour, but preferred playing back on shore. They thought I should learn to swim and, in the summer of fourth grade, registered me at the Elmhurst

YMCA to learn how. Disaster! The instructor forced us to dive off the high dive, and some high-school kid fished us out. Some learned. It left me with a fear of water.

I mostly liked Washington Elementary School, but there I began to see more clearly that I wasn't like most of the other boys. One boy, Phil, from third grade into sixth, called me "little girl" with complete contempt. I never responded, afraid he'd wallop me, afraid I'd rile God if I fought back. "A soft answer turneth away wrath," my mom and church people claimed.

I did have crushes on girls in grade school. Kara sat behind me in fourth grade, and I liked her a lot though she liked to make fun of me. Sometimes love doesn't mind that kind of response. I don't know if I wanted a girlfriend the way Opie wanted Sharon Porter on *The Andy Griffith Show*, or if I just wanted Kara to be my friend. When she threw ink for her cartridge pen at me, my young ardor cooled. She moved away by fifth grade, anyway.

Meg was my favorite in the first part of fifth grade, followed by Jayne in the second half. I liked Jayne more but remember her less. Meg was cute and bright, while Jayne was dark blond, heavier, quieter. Meg was funny. Jayne listened. I hope Jayne and Meg grew up to have interesting lives. A crush doesn't always fizzle completely. A few cells of it may keep floating in my blood.

When I think of boys back then, I can't remember many crushes. Since boys often posed a threat, I didn't fixate on any one too much. Alan was cute with his brown hair. A little shorter than me, he didn't make as much noise as some of the other boys, and at least to my face he never called me "little girl." We were in a few grades together. One day, I lined up behind him and wanted to press myself against him. I never wanted to do that with Jayne or Meg. In junior high, I realized that I wouldn't have minded pressing up against many Alans—and no Meg.

Hormones starting poking holes in the wall of innocence I lived behind. The TV shows I watched never suggested kids felt sexual in any way beyond an "Aw shucks, Wally likes Mary Ellen" way. Kids like me didn't exist on TV—every single one of them would grow up straight, get married, and have kids. Even Eddy Haskell. Well, Zelda Gilroy on *The Many Loves of Dobie Gillis* pined after Dobie, but she didn't seem like the cream-puff girls Dobie usually mooned over. Zelda, way too bright, not perky-pretty, more at ease in a book than a beauty parlor, might not fit with those other TV kids.

Sometimes my older relatives would grin and ask, "Do you have a girlfriend, Kenny?" I'd say no. We'd move on to other subjects. They assumed I would grow up and procreate like the TV character kids: I came from Villa Park, I was a nice boy. Nice boys get married and have kids, and those kids would do the same. A pleaser, I tried to make my family and neighbors happy and proud. I sure tried to please Jesus.

At five, I started going to the Bible Church of Villa Park with my mother. Only four blocks up Villa Avenue, it was originally an old mansion, not a church. But in 1972, church members and others scraped enough money together. Pastor Blunk told us that "debentured bonds," were a safe reason to invest in a new building to replace the leaky mansion-church). My mother had just "accepted Jesus as her own personal Savior." Witnessing for Jesus started at home. My dad, a scientist, would have none of it but didn't interfere with her choice. We'd pray on our knees beside their bed for my dad's soul. She never dressed expensively, wore minimal makeup, and a thin necklace on special occasions or to church. My dad wore dark, baggy pants, never smelled of cologne, rubbers when it rained. They never worried about impressing others.

I started with Sunday School lessons—Bible stories told with coloring books for kids to crayon David, Saul, Paul, Jonah inside the whale. Those were the supporting cast; Jesus got the lead role, always.

Sometimes politics sneaked into the love of God. Sitting on green-painted wooden chairs, Mrs. Sanders, whose son was in Vietnam, told us she thought God wanted us in that war. Mr. Peterson, my Sunday School teacher for a few years, wanted to talk about the Republican Party as much as about sacrificing everything for Jesus. I didn't know any Democrats in our church. It was never stated directly, but God was very American. White American. The picture of Jesus in the Sunday School was blond. He had mournful, gentle brown eyes.

Our headline read God loved "everybody," but the story had some qualifiers. God was easily angered. At missteps, the kindly brown-eyed Jesus would snarl and threaten. We were always in danger of "falling away." Yes, He'd forgive you—if you asked nicely and sincerely—but danger followed us. The world made us into hell's kindling. In church, the other boys didn't call me "little girl." The perennial narrator in the Christmas play, my voice came from a hidden place. My mother, feeling it was her duty even though she hated doing it, often directed. Mrs. Sanders said I sounded like Linus.

I believed it all. Jesus was God. Hell was for unbelievers who would get tossed in fire when they died. Heaven had a place for me. And my mother. But not my dad. God loved him, too, but he wouldn't repent, so hell owned him. My grandparents in Elmhurst were Christian Scientists, a perversion of the "true" Christ, according to Pastor. We had the truth because we knew how to interpret the Bible. So they wouldn't be in Heaven with us, either.

John Stendo was Catholic, another perversion. We didn't need some Vatican guy interceding for us. His sister Mary died at twelve of an enlarged heart. I hadn't known anyone close to my age who had died. I could not accept that she would be in Hell because of the "perversion." I never asked Pastor if Mary's soul made it to heaven for fear of what he might say. I kept my questions neatly wrapped and put away behind my good shoes. Someday God would answer all questions. A "spirit-filled" Christian wouldn't have many questions anyway—as we heard week after week in church: "The Bible says it. I believe it. That settles it."

Pastor and my Sunday school teachers didn't dabble much in talking about sex. You had sex after you got married and didn't have sex with anyone else after that. Sometimes in his sermons, Pastor would allude to adulterers and homosexuals. Of course, these shared the same seat in a burning rowboat. Like my dad, they were tinder, too.

In Villa Park, I had nobody to ask about sex. My dad never sat me down for the birds-and-the-bees talk, which, as it turned out, would have been fairly irrelevant since I would have needed to know if male bees sometimes preferred other male bees. My sex education came from neighborhood boys after I turned thirteen in the late 1960s. I sensed that talking about sex with an adult was a line I wasn't supposed to cross, so I didn't. Maybe people were experimenting in Haight-Asbury, but on Villa Avenue, even masturbation was a sin and not discussable. People could talk about sports (endlessly). Music. TV. Films. Church. Current events. But not sex. Not pleasure.

A friend from school taught me how to masturbate. During a game of hide-and-seek, we hid, and, after some horseplay and nervous chatter, unzipped our pants. I knew I wasn't supposed to do this with him even though nobody directly said so. I felt terrible guilt. Pleasure followed by "Dear Jesus, I'm sorry I fell from your ways once again. Please forgive me and give me the strength to follow you."

Inevitably, I would "fall." My fantasies didn't include girls in my class or film stars. I pictured boys in my class, sometimes in my church, naked. I tried to switch my fantasies to females, but they would drift back to males. Film stars and sports stars rarely did much for me, then or now. An occasional musician would interest me, but the music excited me more than the body.

Jackson Junior High School, a horror literally from day one. In gym class, I dreaded that I would have to undress, dress and shower with other boys. We picked up our uniforms, which included a sealed box holding a jock strap. I had never seen one or worn one before. Naturally, when I tried to wear it, I put it on backwards, thinking the larger part should cover my behind. The network of junior high cruelty immediately sent the message of my jock strap story up and down the halls.

With adolescence, I got gawky, my face broke out, and my parents still picked out my clothes. I hated when I'd have to get new pants—my dad would have to feel around my waist to make sure I had enough "healthful" room to grow. New styles didn't impress my parents. I didn't fight them too much on clothes, but at school I got razzed so badly about my crew cut (completely uncool by 1968) that on a tearful ride to the barber shop, I told my dad to please not make me get another crew cut. He turned the car around, headed home, saying, "A sick generation!"

I still had crushes on girls, or at least one girl, Martha. We loved The Monkees.

Perhaps I loved Mike Nesmith, the Monkee with the wool hat, and she was just the avenue to travel to him. But in the locker room I noticed the boys, especially those who were already a little hairy. I tried not to look, but the garden was too inviting. I learned ways of looking without anyone else knowing. By the end of junior high, everywhere I looked I saw hot guys. Jesus would have to glue my eyes shut, but even then my mind would imagine them. Pray, pray. Boys, boys.

Phil's family moved away, so no one called me "little girl" anymore. I had graduated to faggot and homo. The one hope was to get home, my transistor radio playing WLS or WCFL, The Mamas and The Papas, Donovan, and the ever-faithful Tommy James escorting me from the doorways of junior high hell.

Tell a teacher? Nope. Mom and Dad. Yeah, right. I put my clothes on in the morning, ate breakfast, and went to school.

To this day, school remains a horror for many budding gay kids. One poem I wrote remembers Fred C. Martinez, a gay Native-American kid, savaged and killed in Colorado. Whenever I go back to Villa Park, I walk—incessantly. One of my walks takes me back to Jackson Junior High and to Willowbrook High School. I don't know what, or who, I want to find on these walks. Even after thirty-six years, Jackson doesn't look, from the outside, all that different. Maybe my adult self is looking for my adolescent self, to shield him, to talk to him.

Willowbrook High School did not resemble a TV show like *Happy Days*. My four years there had some happy days and silly moments but also continuous fear. I didn't want high school to be a longer repeat of junior high. I made a couple of friends—both of whom turned out to be gay, though we hadn't come out at the time. We never talked about sex, yet I think we suspected we might be gay. We minded our parents, didn't drink or smoke. I'm still friends with one of those kids, Alex. I'm glad he was there. He had been harassed from grade school on. Now that he lives in Arizona and I live in Pennsylvania, we exchange monthly letters but didn't come out to each other until our late twenties. He told me in a letter with the phrase "Shock Special" written on the envelope. By then, relief replaced shock since I wrote him back and came out, too.

In high school, I knew more fully that I was gay but still clung to the old bromide that "the right girl" would change me. That thinking didn't translate into wild hunts for dates. I didn't date. I wanted "the right girl" to land from Mars, scoop me up, hetero-ize me, and all would be well. I continued to masturbate with the kid who taught me how, in awe of his dick, his hairiness. And pray as I did, I wanted to touch him and have him touch me. He imagined girls. I had him beside me—not imagining girls—fully enjoying him. We never kissed—that would have made us gay. We could continue to do what we wanted "as long as we don't love each other." Queers fell in love with each other. Sex was separate from that.

Gym class remained grim yet less awful than in junior high. Some of my high school classes proved to be useful—like Mr. Stemke's "American Minority Lit." We didn't read any openly gay authors, but we studied works by many marginalized peoples. A door started to open. Because of Mr. Stemke's course, when I became a college teacher, I designed a similar course which I now teach.

Sadly, doors remained closed in the Villa Park Public Library. A good library houses differing opinions on neighboring shelves. Not then. The few books I found on homosexuality said "God doesn't like it." Other perspectives weren't welcome. In fairness, when I was a teenager, fewer books were published on coming out and self-acceptance issues for gays. I didn't read Weinberg's *Society and the Healthy Homosexual* until the late 1970s when I had moved away to do graduate work in English and Creative Writing at the University of Wisconsin in Milwaukee.

I started to write poetry before my junior year started. I wanted to be a pop singer, knew I couldn't sing, but still practiced in front of a mirror singing into a potato masher. I wrote my first poem, "The Open Door," while I sat alone in our basement, a chair pulled up to the ping-pong table, a blank sheet before me. It had peace and love lyrics, exhorting everyone with the immortal line, "C'mon, let's unlock our minds." I thought I was writing about brotherhood. Maybe I knew so much inside me was locked up, including my identity, I needed to walk through an open door to my real self. The doors still felt locked. Tight.

My early poems about Illinois often dripped with bile, nasty critiques of suburbia and greed. I rhymed—badly. I didn't yet even have the words to explore and expose my gay identity. I wrote few love poems, none to another guy.

As in junior high, I listened to music every day, though I fast became disenchanted with the hits of the early seventies and drifted more to WJJD, the country station. I still adored Tommy James, but now I had Sonny James, too. And Jack Blanchard & Misty Morgan. And Dolly Parton. Country or pop, lyricists framed love songs in heterosexual terms, but I unbuckled the lyrics to accommodate gay fantasies. I still do. For all the talk of "do your own thing" in the late sixties and early 1970s, I couldn't do mine. Rock and country music had the same inflexibility as church. The rebellion really meant single straight males wanted to lay single straight women. I had no place in the "rebellion."

I tried to look more cool than the nerd I felt I was, wore bell bottoms, grew my hair longer, and when I got old enough to need to shave (I was a slow bloomer), I added stringy sideburns to the picture. My yearbook pictures showed a blond teenager with thick glasses. High school was larger than junior high; our 1972 graduating class had over 800 kids—I could hide more easily.

I regret how I treated a kid named Mark my freshman year. He even out-nerded me. The gym-class boys went after him with the usual "Fuckin' faggot!" insults that of course no gym teacher ever seemed to hear. Rather than stand up for him, I joined in the laughter, hoping to become less of a target. It worked, somewhat. I felt like crap. And I prayed, yet again, that God would forgive me for being unkind. For all the "peace and good/brotherhood" lyrics of popular songs, we had little peace, did each other too little good, and brotherhood was a nice term for clique.

My school years occurred during an intense period in American history. In Bergman's *Persona*, Elisabeth Vogler, played by Liv Ullman, undergoes hospitalization because she suddenly goes mute on stage. In her hospital room, on TV, she sees a Buddhist monk burn himself up to protest war and violence. Ullmann's face cracks in horror even as she cannot verbally articulate what she feels. Her doctor tells her that, try as she might, reality creeps in. She has no way of blocking it despite her fierce silence.

In our living rooms, body bags. Death counts. Assassinations. Protests. We had lawns to mow, groceries to shop for, church functions to attend. Reality kept seeping in.

My family supported the war for several years. We believed in "the domino effect" (how strange that term sounds now) and feared that we were essentially a rice paddy or two away from being overrun by Communists. Most people over thirty on our street saw the protesters as, at best, misguided and naive; at worst, traitors.

Our open windows brought arguments next door between John's older brother, Dave, and his dad to us. Many Villa Parkers had a big fear of "our" neighborhoods being taken over by African-Americans. Martin Luther King, Jr. was not a hero to many on our street. We had no people of color on our block, hardly any in our town.

Women's issues got scant notice on our block. Most of the adults loathed long hair on males—it suggested a challenge to gender roles. Girls had long hair. Period. The moptop Beatles looked cute, the Sgt. Pepper Beatles a threat. Yet as the kids got older, more moms, including mine, got jobs. Mrs. Stendo took a factory job. Until three years after I moved to Milwaukee, my mother remained a housewife. In 1980, she took a job at the Easter Seals Center, riding her bike to work about six blocks away. On our street, most considered a word like "feminism" goofy and dismissed feminists as "Oh, a bunch of bra burners."

When gays got a mention at all, they were "faggots" or "queers" who most certainly did not live in Villa Park, but probably in cities or out in California where, as one neighbor said, "They're all nuts and fruits." If a woman burned her bra, maybe she was a lesbian, yet another reason to dismiss anything she might have to say.

My parents were Republicans. My father loathed LBJ's "Great Society" ideas. I was a Republican, too, and when Nixon got in, I was happy. I believed in "Peace with Honor," his 1972 campaign slogan. However, by 1972 my family had pretty well moved away from supporting the war. Reality had crept in too much. We had no more hiding places. Blood ran everywhere.

A town or a street can't stay the same. Like me, a late bloomer, some places take longer to change, particularly if little new information seeps in. Despite the many offensive attitudes, I felt safe when I was on my street and in my home. I was loved. During those walks I take, perhaps I'm looking for that security again. I don't want parts of Villa Park to change. When I walk uptown, I stand before brick stores where, on the sides of the building, I can barely make out the faded names of those stores from the 1950s and 1960s. A painted advertisement for the Two Sisters Dress Shop faded into old brick. When the Ovaltine factory closed in the eighties, it sat dormant for about ten years. Windows got busted. It looked like a red-faced dowager, down on her luck, no one left to recognize her.

After high school, I went to Wheaton College, three towns away, an Evangelical institution, the same college that Billy Graham attended. Drive past there now, and you'll see the Graham Center. I stayed at home rather than live in the dorms, so I did not leave Villa Park. I clung to her skirts.

Wheaton had rules I signed onto—no drinking, no dancing, no premarital sex. The premarital sex part assumed marriage would eventually be an issue for horny young Christians. I still gave lip service to the notion that "the right girl" would "fix" me. We had required chapel. I had to take a course called "Christ and Culture" in my freshman year—along with ROTC.

Thursday morning, I lined up in a uniform for a junior to "inspect" me with cold, blue eyes. I tried to escape ROTC by claiming I was against war (which was true), but the school required my Pastor's letter stating he knew of my anti-war views. I didn't want to ask him, fearing I'd get a lecture on why God wants us in Vietnam. He already called my faith "weak."

Young people often experiment in college, the escape from home and hometown offering possibilities for sexual play and discovery. I spent four years on ice with no chance to thaw. To become myself, to finally drop the phony "right girl" notion and claim my identity as a gay person, I had to leave—to get free of Wheaton College and Villa Park. It's not that I was always unhappy in either place. I had some good classes. At home, I got involved in gardening, an interest I cherish to this day. Villa Park kept me small and contained. Wheaton nurtured that smallness.

Cracks began to form in the ice. After her father died an unbeliever, my mother started to move away from her fundamentalist beliefs. I finally starting meeting more kids I could be friends with—not open with, but at least it was a start. At school, I met other students who also wanted to write. One friend, a young poet, and I clicked. My fundamentalism paled in comparison with hers. Her folks had been missionary doctors in Panama. In my senior year, she introduced me to St. Barnabas Episcopal Church which I attended for two years, a small but important step away from the Bible Church. That same year, the man who would become my Ph.D. advisor in Wisconsin came for a short appointment at Wheaton. A poet, he gave me specific feedback on my poems and suggested I consider UWM for graduate school.

While in college, I worked for a while as a Holiday Inn houseboy (shampooing carpets, dumping trash) and then as a busboy at Stouffer's Hotel and Restaurant in Oakbrook, three miles from home. The working world was much different from the one I entered at Wheaton each day. Before "Q Time," when our floor leaders told us the daily specials, I would sit and talk with the waitresses or the busboys, most of whom still attended high school. I heard fun gossip about sex and drugs. Waitresses often left cigarette packs in the back room. I snuck cigarettes, found I enjoyed smoking despite warnings against it. I got hooked and it took me almost thirteen years to get free. Some waitresses talked about their love lives and boyfriend situations. Emily had many boyfriends. Agnes had one she would marry in a Catholic ceremony. I had nothing to add to the love chatter. While I had signed a pledge not to fornicate, I found these fornicators much more interesting. I had a slight crush on one busboy, Stu, but he kept whining about finding girls. I had a crush on a hotel clerk, but he talked just like Stu. I didn't know of any gay employees other than me. Perhaps, like me, they kept snug in their closets, at least to themselves.

I kept working at Stouffer's and lived at home during the year after I graduated Wheaton. My mom remembers this time fondly. We often ate lunches together and took bike rides to resale shops. I applied to UWM and got accepted. Attendance there would finally get me out of Villa Park and into a city. I wanted and didn't want to go. Our street had not physically changed much. The Dutch Elm trees of my childhood had gotten diseased and died, so smaller trees grew where the elms had once formed a protective canopy over us. I needed to be less protected, too.

When I had the car packed and ready, my parents looked very sad, my mother especially. I had to get well on the highway before I cried. I hadn't fully accepted that my childhood life had ended so an adult life could begin. I kept moving forward, passed the Wisconsin welcome sign. My Toyota entered Milwaukee.

George Burns writes that when someone played vaudeville, if the owners didn't like your act, they fired you by giving you your pictures back. You took them with you to the next job, handed them to someone who might give you a chance, and hoped. My act was over. Fresh out of Ovaltine, I gave Villa Park its pictures back. I was finally ready to taste my future.

Waking Up in Fifth Grade

Alan Witchey

Phillip Todd and I spent afternoons fighting alien invaders, catching garden snakes from the wood pile, and building forts in the woods across from our homes. We had been friends for three years, but in fifth grade, a burning desire filled me to touch him in a new way, to caress his body. I remember becoming acutely aware of it in the autumn. We lay on the dry leaves in the large wooded area surrounding Franke Park in Fort Wayne, Indiana. Gray clouds rolled overhead, and the air was humid. Hundreds of naked branches crisscrossed the sky above us as we searched for shapes – a hobby we'd started several weeks prior. Phillip had spotted a pouncing lion and a dog.

"Brontosaurus," he traced the long neck with thick fingers.

I scooted in close to him, searching for the dark lines that formed the prehistoric beast. I tried to concentrate on finding the creature, but having his body so close to mine made the lines blur together. Focusing on the way his finger traced the shape over and over again I found it and nodded. The branches formed a dinosaur as though the trees were silent artists.

"Cool," I said, admiring its perfect form. "How can that happen?"

"It's about letting your mind see the world differently."

His mind was able to spot these miraculous figures while mine could only confirm his discoveries. I felt the need to find one myself, to show Phillip that I too had the mental capability of seeing the world's magic. The dark lines melted in and out of each other as I searched. Reluctantly giving up, I turned my head toward Phillip's small body and watched the way his thin chest raised and fell to the rhythm of his breathing. I became aware of my own breathing and tried to make it match his. When I finally managed to synchronize our inhalations and exhalations, I returned my eyes to the lines in the sky. Then I saw it. The belly curved above us into an enormous tail.

"Whale," I said.

The shape was huge, larger than his dinosaur, but less defined. It was missing a flipper, but he agreed to it. Phillip jumped up, satisfied with our small zoo, and left the branch animals behind. He sprinted ahead, smaller and quicker than I was. His lips twisted slightly when he smiled, and his curly hair blew wildly in the wind. I wore an orange sweatshirt that Phillip said made me look like I was going hunting.

"I wish," I admitted. "I'd hunt black panthers in Africa."

"Rhinoceros," he corrected me. "When you eat their horns, it heals anything wrong with you."

Would it cure me, I wondered, from wanting to kiss him? I felt as though all people were normal except me. I wanted Phillip in the same way other boys wanted girls. I had always felt different, but now it was more pronounced. When I got old enough, I vowed to go to Africa to find one of these horns and eat it.

"Let's be hunters," Phillip suggested.

"In the African jungle," I said.

I picked up a stick with a V shape in the end that created a handle – my rifle. Phillip searched the ground and found a smaller but adequate replica to act as his rifle and began to search the forest for hidden rhinoceroses. Dark-rooted tree trunks – oaks, maples, sycamores, and pines – stretched into the distance for acres. Our prey could be hiding ten feet out in front of us, and we'd never see them. Phillip made several shooting sounds, and I followed his lead.

"I got one," he said.

"Me too."

We jumped onto our pretend carcasses, using our sticks now as knives, and stabbed them over and over again. At last, the beasts lay dead beneath us. We sawed the invisible horns off with great effort and held them above our heads.

"We'll live forever if we eat these," he said. The horns' powers shifted from healing illness to granting immortality, a transition I accepted without question.

"Forever together," I cried as we gobbled them up.

We shook our arms and legs, hopping and screaming erratically: Becoming eternal beings required a physical transformation. When we were done, I felt happy knowing that I would see Phillip Todd for the rest of my life. We continued on our journey, searching for other African beasts.

"My family's going to Florida in a week," he said. "I get to miss school."

Phillip had never mentioned the trip before. An empty feeling filled my heart as I imagined a week without seeing him. We'd been separated for that long before, but now it felt different. I would feel dead without him in my life for a week.

"It'll be weird not to see you for that long," he said.

A tingling rush filled me as I realized he'd miss me. His arm rubbed against mine as we walked along the narrow path. I moved closer to him.

"Nichole Baker is hot," he said. "I'd like to fuck her tight pussy."

"She screams like a hyena," I said. "Billy Johnson screwed her."

"Alan, Billy Johnson's a faggot ape."

Phillip hunched over and curved his arms up to his sides like a chimpanzee. Hooting like a monkey, he catapulted himself onto a low tree branch and swung while making deep grunts. I applauded. He flung himself from the branch into my body, clasping his arms around my waist and throwing his weight against mine, sending us both tumbling into the blanket of decaying leaves. We rolled, and I ended up on top of him pinning his arms to the ground. He struggled to break free, but I was stronger. I had him trapped. I imagined kissing him, feeling the warmth of his lips to mine. I wanted him to be my Nichole Baker.

"Let me up."

I climbed off of him. Bits of brown clung to his green shirt as we stood. He walked bowlegged, a feature I mimicked, not to ridicule him but to be more like him. I wanted to feel those legs wrap around my back as I lay between them.

"I'm going to ask Nichole Baker to a movie next Saturday," he said.

"Don't bother. I'll go with you," I said.

"I want to go with her."

"Why?" I asked.

"Boys ask girls to the movies."

"You want to screw her," I accused.

"She's pretty."

Nichole had long, brown hair and beautiful, smooth skin. She wore dresses every day and smelled of flowers. She took delicate steps as though she was never in a hurry. Would he find me attractive if I acted like her? A flush of jealousy filled me as I pictured the two of them holding hands in the movie theater.

"You going to pay her way?" I asked.

"Got to on a date."

Phillip wanted her, not me. I felt the urge to scream, but I held it in – stuffed it deep into the rotting carcasses of a hundred other desires that I had smothered. It was a dank, moldy place where my yearnings for Phillip and other men were chained to the walls.

The path exited along the small gravel road that led into the park, and a clearing next to it contained a faded picnic table. Phillip and I came out of the trail to see a blue Pontiac with giant rust spots curved around the tires and coated in a thin layer of dust. No one was in the picnic area, and the car was empty, abandoned. I wondered if a man had murdered his wife and left her body to rot where no one would find it for weeks.

Phillip put his finger to his lips. He bent down and crawled to the car on his hands and knees. I shook my head and motioned for him to come away. My throat constricted, and my heart began pumping harder. Phillip was about to discover a dead body, and we had no idea if the murderer was hiding nearby. Phillip popped his head up and peered in through the car window. His body teetered and retreated back down. He turned to me with a fully extended smile. He wobbled back and forth using one hand to balance himself.

He motioned his arm for me to approach. If it were a dead body, he wouldn't have smiled. There was something else. I crawled toward him, stepping carefully to avoid the crunch of dead leaves. Next to each other, I breathed deeply smelling his sweet body odor. He had the faint scent of soap. I had an urge to push my lips against his again. It was instinctual, and I had to consciously stop myself. He would never allow it.

"Look," he mouthed silently.

We slowly rose. Inside was a couple in their thirties. The man had a dark moustache and smooth legs, and the woman had long red hair and a perky nose. They lay snaked around each other, both of their jeans pushed down to their ankles, revealing their naked bodies. The couple looked ordinary, any couple I might have seen at the movie theater or at the grocery store, except that their faces were buried in each other's crotches. I felt an electric pulse run through me as I watched them engrossed in their rhythmic actions – the man's tongue rapidly entering and exiting the woman's hairy slit, her mouth bobbing up and down on his veiny cock. Goosebumps covered my arms.

"Jackpot," whispered Phillip.

Their bodies weaved in and out of each other making it difficult to distinguish what body parts were his and which ones were hers. I found the couple strangely beautiful in their motion. I wanted to erase her from the scene, so I could focus on his fleshy arms, his muscled legs, and his erection. But she was there, creating a scene I was supposed to want: one man, one woman. I felt drawn to the woman's mouth moving up and down. Her eyes were closed, and a strange satisfied expression covered her face. His shirt was pushed up, and her hand was rubbing a small patch of dark hair on his chest. I wanted to be her, to touch a man in the same way. I had pictured it hundreds of times in my mind, but I had gotten it all wrong. The way the man's body arched with pleasure at her strokes and the relaxation on his face. Not relaxation, but something I hadn't yet discovered: ecstasy. I wanted to make men feel that way.

Phillip and I watched for five or six minutes, both of us bulging in our pants. My legs were shaking. The urge to reach out and touch Phillip grew stronger. We stood so close that I could hear his heavy breaths. I found myself taking secret side-glances at Phillip, first memorizing the expression on his face and then staring at the obvious tent in his groin.

The man's penis was huge, and I was impressed that the woman could swallow it entirely. I relaxed my throat muscles and wondered if I could consume its length or if I would gag. What did it taste like? Did the man smell as sweet as Phillip did? The woman pulled her shirt up to reveal her breasts, and Phillip elbowed me. She opened her eyes and shifted, as though to pull away from her lover. We ducked back down and crawled away. Backtracking along the path, we planned to come back onto the road further down.

Phillip said, "Saw a real pussy."

"Sure hairy," I said.

"Bet it tasted good."

"Like honey," I said. "They taste like honey." I was making it up, but Phillip nodded in agreement.

"I wish I was that guy," he confessed.

"Me too."

In truth, I wished that I could be a woman. That was the only way I could imagine I would ever be able to caress a man. I would need to grow my own breasts, to lose my dick – then I would feel normal. If I grew long, feminine fingers I would be allowed to run them over Phillip's chest or through his hair. I wanted to fall to my knees in front of him and take him in my mouth the way I saw the woman doing. I tried to find some hint of recognition, some minor cue that would allow me to reach out and touch him. I wanted to let him know that it was okay for him to rub his hand on my chest. Then for a second, the thought seemed to flicker through his mind, too. I could read the lust in his face that cared only to get off.

All I had to do was place my hand on him, take the lead. No one would see us in the woods. No one would know. Getting him off would be nothing more than getting lost in the moment. He could still be normal if he let me blow him when a woman got him excited. A deep apprehension held me still. Would he reject me? If I were misreading his lust, our friendship would be over. More than that, he would tell everyone at school that I was a faggot. If I didn't act, I would never get the chance again. I leaned in closer. His breath smelled of mint. I wanted to taste it. His hand wavered near his crotch, uncertain whether he should touch it.

As I looked into Phillip's eyes, I knew he wanted me in the same way I wanted him. I tried to speak but made some base animal noise. I didn't want it to be a mindless carnal act; I wanted it to be a gentle experience. I wanted to curl up with him, to hold his hand, to tell him that I loved him. But there could be no words for what we were considering. Time stretched from seconds to minutes. He turned his head and took a step away.

Phillip began talking about the woman's pussy again. I had waited too long. We walked in silence for several minutes. I thought I was corroded, worthless, or malfunctioning. Phillip was stimulated by the woman, like every other boy in the world would be. I was alone in my feelings of attraction to men. I felt defective, as though the fibers of my body had been wired incorrectly. I pictured the man's tongue bobbing in and out of the pussy. I would change, become normal by thinking over and over about the woman.

Phillip led us out of the woods and back onto the road. Trees covered most of Franke Park's 300, but a central clearing had a large pond and a playground with steel monkey bars, a giant swing set, a merry-go-round, a volleyball tied to a tall metal pole, and a large cement turtle surrounded by sand. This was our kingdom, a walking distance of fifteen minutes from our homes. There were several other kids on the playground – three were holding desperately to the merry-go-round as an older man in green slacks spun it.

"The tit," I said. That was our nickname for the merry-go-round, which had a strange nipple-like protrusion from its center.

"I'd love to suck a nipple that big," said Phillip.

"Couldn't fit in your mouth," I said.

"I'd be happy to roll on it. To smell like a giant tittie."

We went to the steel tower of monkey bars. The bottom level was a large rectangle of five-by-eight cubes, each level becoming increasingly reduced, so that the fifth and uppermost level had only two cubes. That was where we were headed. When I touched the metal, it was cold, frozen. I pulled my sweatshirt sleeves over my hands and began climbing.

"Beat you to the top," I said.

"You could only beat your little sister."

We pounced from bar to bar focusing on the final target. My foot slipped, sending one leg into the air, but I threw my body upward and pulled myself onto the next level with only my hands. Phillip laughed at my mistake, using the split-second advantage to put him in the lead. But I knew a trick. I got my feet balanced again and propelled my body up another level – just enough to allow me to win. I crowed victory with one hand waiving in the air.

"I let you win," he said.

"You never let anyone win," I said.

"I felt sorry for you. That was your first time to see a naked woman."

"I've seen plenty."

"Your sister doesn't count," he pushed me lightly.

"I saw Nichole Baker when I screwed her."

"You said Billy Johnson screwed her."

"Both did. Shared her."

"That would be so cool," he said.

Perched like birds, we could survey the entire park from there. Large willows lined the pond where a group of kids were feeding bread to ducks. Their lives looked so simple from a distance. The wind blew in giant cold gusts around us. I felt free, normal. If I stayed there, I would never have to face being queer. I could do nothing more than stare off into the distance.

High-pitched squeals rose from below. A blond girl, no more than seven, was at the second level and had started to cry. Her pigtails stuck up like antlers on a stag.

"Girls don't belong on monkey bars," Phillip said.

"I can't get down," the girl cried.

Her mother, a tall woman in a pink coat, came to rescue her, coaxing her down slowly, one bar at a time. We giggled, throwing our hands in the air, pretending as though we might fall. Brave, we sat on top of the world; nothing could harm us.

"It's time to go, sweetheart," said the woman.

After she took her daughter to their car, Phillip said, "Sweetheart, it's time for me to suck your pussy."

"She's old," I said.

"Pussy is pussy, Alan. All tastes the same."

"Hers is rotten. Probably dry."

We smirked and high-fived each other. Phillip draped his legs over the top bar and fell backwards, upside down. I mimicked him. As the blood rushed to our heads, uncontrollable fits of laughter flew out of our mouths. We hung there, hooting hysterically. Phillip's shirt slid toward his face, revealing his smooth belly. His bellybutton was beautiful the way it sank. I wanted to touch it, to first explore it with my finger and later fill it with my tongue. I wanted to create an opportunity where we could be alone together, where I could see if he felt the same way.

"Want to spend the night?" I asked.

"School tomorrow."

Phillip was distant. He seemed to be reconsidering staying the night. Maybe he was trying to get up the courage to tell me that he felt the same way. Or had he figured out that I was a faggot and didn't want anything more to do with me?

"Alan, let's go back to that car."

We could watch the couple and get excited again, eventually retreating to the woods. It would go differently this time. I'd be bold and act rather than feebly observe. I greedily agreed. A faint sound of thunder came from the distance.

"Going to rain," I said.

"Pass us by," said Phillip.

We sat up on the bars. I felt lightheaded as the blood pumped back toward my feet. Phillip and I sat, neither one talking, but both connected. His lips were plump and red; the urge to kiss him came back.

The breeze shifted and colder air blew in. We watched as black clouds pushed the gray ones into the east. Lightning lit up the sky. A thundering crash sounded as if it had hit close by, and parents rushed their children to their cars. Enormous raindrops began to hit us. A massive thunderstorm was starting, and we wouldn't have time to get home before getting soaked. We climbed down, as the raindrops got heavier, and searched for protection.

"Shelter," he pointed.

A small brick building with a slate roof and no windows housed the public restroom for the park. It possessed a strange charm with large wide steps at the base leading up to progressively smaller ones. An arched doorway led to a solid steel door. The building looked like a small cottage, as though it had been intended for more than it was being used. In all the times we'd been to the park, we'd never gone inside. In less than a minute, we could be lost in the woods, out of sight, if the need to piss arose. We ran across the grass to our salvation, approaching one side and, after reading the word women, running to the other. The heavy door opened with a loud screech of metal on ceramic tile.

A sour smell filled the room – the stench of piss, shit, mildew, and dirt. There were three stalls, separated by big white bricks, and two urinals with nothing between them. The room was empty except for the two of us. Rain thudded on the roof. Strands of water ran down Phillip's face, his hair flattened by dampness. He was drenched, shivering. I should have been cold too, but standing so close to him warmed me.

"Cold?" I asked.

I stood with my face inches from his, rubbing his arms to warm him. The intimacy of the room got me excited, and, standing so close to Phillip, I was soon erect again. I wanted to strip off our wet clothes, to wrap my arms around his naked body, to comfort him in this rank sanctuary. At first, he welcomed my heated palms, but, as I leaned in closer, an alarm sounded in his mind. An awkward, blank expression crossed his face. Phillip's muscles tightened as he broke away.

"We should go," he said. "We're already wet."

"Give it a few minutes."

Phillip crossed to the far side of the room, stretching to relax. His arching body reminded me of the man's in the car. I wanted to go to him, to rub his chest and his crotch. I wanted to drop his jeans to the floor, to bury his cock in my mouth. He gazed at the walls in a peculiar way. There must have been something there, something that interested him.

"People have written on the walls," he said. "Look at this."

I stood close to him, my body less than an inch away from his, as I read the words. "I will suck your cock Tuesdays at 7:00 PM," was written in black marker. Phillip wrinkled his face as though he were in pain. The words disgusted him. But for me, it was as if we had discovered a valuable historic document. Then to the left was another one, "For a B.J. be here Sunday at 4:00," and below that a crude picture of an erect penis going into a man's mouth. Three or four similar messages, some no more than dates and times, covered the wall.

The mysteries of the universe were unlocked. There were other men who longed to touch each other. And we had stumbled into the place where they met. For the first time, I knew I was not alone.

"Fags," said Phillip. "That's disgusting."

I was silent, reading the phrases over and over again. I wanted to cut them out of the wall, take them home as proof that there were others like me. Phillip gawked, challenging me to denounce the men who had written these phrases. We discovered something critically important to my existence, but I couldn't make sense of it all yet. Was this how I would end up if I became a faggot – secret meetings planned in a public bathroom?

"Sure is," I said. "Damn fags."

"Screw the rain. Let's get the hell out of here."

"Fuck, yes."

Had my words masked their true feeling or did Phillip have some sense that I might be like these people? Phillip glowed – there was nothing ordinary about him. His wet clothes clung tightly to his body, and even though he was drenched, he was beautiful. Reading those words on the wall made me want him more than ever. I didn't want to come to this scary, dank room to find my lover. I wanted it to be Phillip, one of the normal ones, but I knew it would never be.

The door squeaked again when he opened it. We could see only a few feet through the shower of water. I wanted to stay. Maybe one of the men who wrote on the wall would come back. I wouldn't have known what to do if he did. We walked out into the pouring rain, leaving the sacred meeting space. But I would come back. Even as I told myself that I wouldn't, I knew it was a lie. This room was the only place I knew how to make a connection to someone else who felt the way I did.

New Kid in Town

Charles Jensen

Eagle only had two real claims to fame: John Dillinger had passed through town in the 1920s between bank jobs, trying to find a quiet place to lay low; and once, a couple of kids who were digging around in one of Eagle's three big hills found a rough yellow diamond in the dirt. There weren't any stoplights in Eagle, and the traffic that whizzed by was always on its way to somewhere else. Most surprising about the town was its water tower, which neglected to offer a name but was instead painted canary yellow with a big smiley face at the bulby top of its slender neck.

My family lived at the end of a small cul-de-sac with several empty lots overgrown with tall grass that hosted a variety of noisemaking insects. That year, I was practically an only child, my two older brothers both in school at the same college four hours away. I had my own bedroom and access to all the cool stuff they left at home, whatever I wanted to get my hands on. My dad, who until then had worked at home, recently began renting office space downtown from the only lawyer in Eagle.

Andrea lived in the house behind me and was my age. She wasn't born in Eagle—she moved here in first grade, but to me, she always felt like the new kid. I was the one who had to walk her to her first day of school and show her around, which I was kind of excited about and kind of embarrassed about. She seemed really small and meek, all bundled up in a fluffy winter coat with wisps of her fine blond hair sticking out around her hood. After a while, she got mouthy just like the rest of us, and we used to hang out a lot. Her mom was divorced, the only divorced person I ever knew in real life, and didn't watch us very much when we played. Once Andrea and I were going to watch a movie at her house, but the tape we put in was porn. Equally entranced and disturbed, we sat transfixed for about twenty minutes, our preteen hearts pounding, until we were sure we'd get caught and turned it off.

A few weeks into the summer I was playing over at Andrea's house (but not watching porn) and we decided to get some ice cream. J.J.'s Drive-In Restaurant was only about two hundred feet down the road from her house, so we hopped on our bikes and rode over. J.J.'s offered wide, greasy burgers with melted cheese, soft-serve ice cream cones as tall as your head, and crisp fries. It wasn't McDonald's, but the nearest one of those was twenty minutes by car so we made do.

We pulled up our bikes and parked them outside the door to the restaurant, knocking down the kickstands with the toe of our shoes. Neither of us had a bike lock and there wasn't a bike rack to hook them to, anyway. The restaurant had been there as long as I could remember, built at the bottom of Diamond Hill, the place where those kids found the diamond whenever it was. At the top of the hill was the water tower. Part of the hill was dug away or falling down, some broken sod at the top of it with a rain of gravel and rocks rolling down to the back wall of the restaurant's kitchen. Inside, a large rectangular window separated the kitchen from the seating area, which offered about seven brown, yellow, and orange colored-booths. Andrea and I walked up to the window where a blond high school girl was taking orders.

"Large chocolate cone," I told the girl. Andrea ordered the same. The girl turned and placed a wafer cone under the soft-serve nozzle and wound her hand carefully as the ice cream oozed out. She finished the cone with a wrist flourish that tied the tip of the soft serve around the top of the cone. She handed the first one to Andrea and the second one to me. We climbed into a booth. If we sat on our feet, we could see through the window overlooking the two-lane highway we biked to get here and some houses clustered between the highway, the train tracks beyond it. In front of the nearest house, a kid outside was pushing a lawnmower over the grass. He looked like he was our age, maybe a little older. Probably sixth or seventh grade, I thought. He had dark, spiky hair that he kept pushing up as he wiped the sweat from underneath the sweatband on his forehead. His yellow tank-top revealed tanned arms the color of a dirt road on a dry day.

"Who's that guy?" I asked Andrea.

"I don't know, " she said. "I've never seen him before."

"Maybe he's new. Are we getting a new kid at school this year?" I asked this in the most natural way possible, as though it were the kind of thing sixth graders discussed.

"Beats me."

Andrea started talking about something else. I watched the guy walking back and forth in his yard, pushing the mower, shoving it over lumps and rocks in the ground, never pausing. Just walking back and forth, back and forth.

Back at Andrea's after the ice cream, I felt jittery inside, like my skeleton and my skin were suddenly a mismatch and both were trying to outwrestle the other. It was a feeling I didn't have a name for. But I was pretty sure it had something to do with that boy, the lawn-mowing boy. My mind kept returning to him, to the image of his sweaty hair standing straight up, or to the shape of his arm as it gripped the handle of the mower. Andrea pulled out her Barbie dolls.

"I think this Barbie should be a horse rider. I know she likes horses. There, grab that pony over there." She gestured to a horse laying on its side under her little sister's bed.

"I wonder how long he's lived here."

"Who?"

"That kid."

"Oh." She put the Barbie on the horse's back. The Barbie was still completely naked, as they often were when we played. "She's going to ride the horse and teach it how to jump over creeks and logs."

The jitteriness hadn't gone away, but it was soon joined by another feeling. Maybe not a feeling so much as a conclusion. I had to meet the boy, but I couldn't just walk over there because that would be weird, suspicious—although suspicious for what reason I couldn't say. I was nervous about meeting him. The idea itself might have been the source of my jitters, like when you have ten dollars and you're running all over the store looking at everything trying to decide exactly what you should buy with it, trying to use it all in one go because how often do you have ten dollars at once? But Andrea, I thought—she could go over there and it would be okay because girls are always trying to say hi to boys. And I could go with her and kind of hang in the background and offer to be his guy friend, like I'm just with this girl because she was nervous about meeting him. I thought of ways to make it happen.

"I bet he doesn't have any friends. You should go over there and say hi."

Andrea made a sour face. "No way. Boys are dumb. Besides, we're playing Barbies." She finished with a raised tone in her voice that indicated I was surely one of the dumb boys for not noticing we were obviously playing Barbies at this time and were not available to go around meeting people.

I gave up. Sort of. We played Barbies for about twenty minutes—nothing serious, nothing complicated. That Barbie did teach the horse how to jump over creeks while another one moved into the Dream House with two Kens, whom she made do all the housework and home repairs while she lay in bed. When Barbies started to get boring, I brought up the boy again.

"You remember when you moved here and didn't know anyone. I bet he's bored and doesn't have anything fun to do."

Andrea, aggravated, growled. "Fine. We'll go say hi. But only for a minute and then I'm coming back home." She stood up and walked into the kitchen, barely waiting to see if I followed.

I was probably sweating but blamed it on the summer heat. The afternoon sun was starting to color everything into darkening shades of yellow and orange as it set. Andrea and I stood in front of the boy's house, our bikes dropped onto their sides on his lawn. My jitters were at their peak, my hands suddenly gone cold. Andrea knocked on the door.

We waited a few minutes. His house was square and two stories tall. Dark brown stain covered the wood siding. The roof dropped to either side of the front door like hair. We squinted and peered into large front porch through its screen door. The porch was covered with scattered junk: a broken bicycle, a couch with stuff poked through two of the cushions, some wrought-iron fireplace tools covered at the ends with gray ash. I took everything in as quickly as possible, trying to find anything that would give me a clue about who this boy was. My heart beat hard and fast.

After a long minute, a silhouette appeared behind the curtain of the front door and opened it. The boy stepped out onto the front porch with some uncertainty, still wearing the headband, the yellow tank top he'd worn to mow the lawn.

"Who're you?" he said. His voice was lower than mine but not older than mine.

Andrea told him our names. "I'm Jacob," he said.

"We saw you mowing the lawn and wanted to come over and say hi," she continued. "Maybe you could hang out with us sometime."

Jacob was clearly unsure of what to make of us. Close-up, his face revealed thick, dark brown eyebrows over eyes of the same color, chipmunkish cheeks, and when he talked, a tiny chip out of the corner of one of his front teeth.

A dog appeared from around the side of the porch and immediately started barking, its thin jaws snapping shut with each yelp. Jacob sighed and came through the screen door into the yard. The dog kept barking but knew its time was short. He walked up to the dog, grabbed his collar, and brought him back to where we were standing. The barking stopped, but the dog was still concerned about what we were doing in his yard. Half of the dog's nose was missing, a pink scar left behind over the place where the nostril lead into its head. One of its eyes was a regular black dog eye, the other was a watery blue. "This is Blue," Jacob said, "and he's really tame. He just barks a lot. He lost his nose cuz another dog bit it off cuz he wouldn't stop barking at it, but he didn't learn."

"Gross," I said, still jittery, still looking at Jacob, feeling uncontrollably like I wanted him to be my friend, inexplicably, and for a long time.

Later that week, I tried to convince Andrea to go out with him, to be his girlfriend. "No way!" she said over and over. "Why don't you be his girlfriend?" she retorted and laughed. I was frustrated with her. Why wouldn't she like him? He was a nice guy and he...had something. Something about him. If I wanted to be his friend so bad, she should obviously want to go out with him. I didn't understand.

I invited him over to my house a while later. My mom was in the kitchen, probably making cookies or starting to work on stuff for dinner. "This is Jake," I said, because I decided not long after we met that I was going to start calling him Jake. It sounded cooler than Jacob. "Wanna play Nintendo?" I asked.

"Cool! You've got Excitebike!" Jake said when he saw my games. We sat down and started playing, but it wasn't ten minutes later that my mom came in, hands on the sides of her apron, saying, "It's a beautiful day. Go outside! You're going to waste your whole life playing that game." We groaned, and I gave Jake that look that said, God, my mom's so lame, I'm really sorry. We went outside.

Between my house and Andrea's was a tiny grove of oak trees that nobody seemed to own. They grew out of the ground at an angle, from under a strip of concrete that was probably the foundation to a tool shed or other building long gone. In the summer time, the trees grew so full and leafy that they blocked out most of the sun, but more importantly, they blocked out the eyes of just about every adult on the street. Jake and I ducked into the grove and sat down on a thick bough near the base of one of the trees. Another branch ran in front of us at about shoulder level, and we raised our arms and crossed them on the higher branch.

"Where are you from again?" I asked him.

"Wauwatosa," he said. I only sort of knew where it was, a suburb of Milwaukee that I didn't remember ever going to. In short: the big city. "We hadta move cuz my parents got divorced. My dad and my brother and me had to go somewhere else because my mom still lives in our old house."

I nodded like I understood how hard it was. Jake was wearing another tank top, and under the shoulder of his crossed arms I noticed a shadow, which turned out to be the first sprouts of dark hair growing there. The jitters returned and my head started swimming. Jake was so cool, I kept telling myself. He's the kind of guy I want to be.

It was afternoon and already midsummer. I could sense the way the days were turning back towards school, to early mornings and packed lunches and recesses. Jake was a year younger than me and wouldn't be in my class. I was disappointed, but I knew I'd still see him at school. And besides, he just lived down the road.

"Shoot!" Jake yelled, grabbing the branch with both hands and swinging under it.

"What's wrong?" I asked. He was already walking out from under the trees.

"I hafta get home, I almost forgot!" he said over his shoulder.

I didn't know what was happening, so I just followed him until I caught up. He was walking fast, stiffly, trying to move as fast as possible without actually running. "What's going on?" I asked again.

"It's nothing, it's just...I hafta get home. You can come if you want, but..." His voice trailed off. I kept pace with him until we were back at his house, walking into the dark front porch with all its junk, and finally into the kitchen.

Jake went into the pantry and grabbed a box of generic macaroni and cheese, then filled a pan near the sink with water and poured the macaroni in it, putting it on the stove to boil. "I forgot I hafta make dinner before my dad gets home or he'll get mad. I always forget to make dinner." He looked at the clock. It was just after five. "I think I can get it done. He has to pick up my brother from day care."

I looked around Jake's house. The kitchen was small and dark at this time of day, having no windows that faced the sunset. There were dirty dishes scattered around the sink. No sign of a dishwasher. The dining room table was made out of thin strips of wood and only had three matching chairs. The fourth was a crooked metal folding chair covered with a Star Wars bed sheet.

I didn't know what to say. I had never made dinner for my family before, and I was even older than he was. I wanted to tell him something that would make him feel better, that would make him feel like we were close friends. Instead, I just stood there and watched.

When the macaroni boiled, Jake grabbed it from the stove, spilling some of the water. The pan dripped as he held it over the sink with two hands, trying to pour the water out without losing the macaroni. "Shit," he swore, and quickly turned around and looked at me to see if I reacted. I never swore before, but I knew people who did so it didn't matter to me. "I can't get the water out," he hissed, and his voice sort of broke. His shoulders were shaking. "Shit!" he said again, putting the pan down on the other side of the split sink. I walked over and followed his look at the sink drain. It was nearly covered with macaroni and water was pooling at the bottom of the sink. "I hafta get this cleaned up, but the macaroni's too hot to touch."

I grabbed a couple of paper towels from a nearby roll and handed them to him. He looked at me gratefully and started to pick at the macaroni. When it got too far into the sink drain for him to reach, he pushed it through the drain, slicing up the noodles as they pushed through the grate. He dropped some butter and poured a little milk into the pan and started stirring quickly. I handed him the cheese packet and he dumped that on top, turning the whole mess a sickly dark orange. "You'd better go," Jake said.

"Do you need help? I can help you," said, thinking of ways I could help. I didn't want to go. There was a feeling in me that I still hadn't learned the name for, but the name didn't matter. I was feeling it when Jake was around—even when he wasn't around and I was just thinking about hanging out with him. It was a need. It was a widening space that was opening inside of my body that only knew one thing: what was missing. Before I saw him mowing the lawn that day, I was just a boy. But now, after knowing him, I was something more complicated. Something a little less complete.

"No, you'd better go," he repeated, his back to me as he stirred the mac and cheese. I stood there for another moment watching him, watching the sky through the window behind him turn darker blue. I heard the sound of gravel crunching under tires in the driveway. Before Jake could turn around to tell me to go, I slipped out the front door and walked back towards my house. As I stepped off Jake's lawn, I looked back at his house. Blue was running around the driveway, yapping at nothing, excited about the arrival of his dad's pick-up. I saw that the kitchen light was on. And then, I was too far to see his house at all.

Their American Dream

Nancy Dempsey

I marvel at the majesty of one-hundred-year-old oaks as I drive down this street that is named for a Confederate general. My new friend has invited me over to meet the wife and child and to help me with some research I am doing. I am instructed, "Check out number 404. We just closed on it yesterday. We need more room now."

Number 404 is a massive, grey-stoned, three-story family home, circa 1900's that, I am told, has a fountain in the garden out back, and a huge yard, with plenty of room for the children to play, and two offices, so my friend's wife can now have her own.

My own mother grew up a few miles from here, in another stone house, where her father, a successful purveyor of stone and tile masonry showcased his handiwork. As I look at the marble stairs and the stone houses that line the block, I wonder how much of this work my grandfather's father might have done in his young apprentice years as I know that he was a stone and marble mason and painter during the time when many of these homes were erected. I feel family history close, and picture my red-haired mother as a child, running up and down the sidewalk. I will think of her again, when, upon my entering through the massive glass front door, my friend's five-year-old daughter dashes down a winding staircase, her cheeks flushed from the summer heat, her bare feet skipping across the rug until she spots me, the stranger, gets shy, turns tail and runs back up the stairs.

Perhaps she senses that I am here to learn the story of her birth and of her parents' history together. I have come in search of their stories, stories that seem so improbable to be occurring in this traditional Southern place, where things seem to change both quickly and slowly simultaneously. On this street, nothing appears to have changed in one hundred years, unless you note the Saabs and SUV's in the driveways, instead of horses and carriages, and, of course, the street is now paved. And this home, with its beautiful antiques and nod to the craftsman era, is comfortable, inviting, and I sink into the luxuriously cushioned sofa and immediately relax.

We have been chatting for awhile when my friend's wife calls down from the staircase, "I'll be there in a minute!"

"Lee, I cannot believe you did not offer Nancy anything to drink or eat!" Anita chastises my friend with her soft drawl in a manner that reminds me of my own mother's. She is still in her church dress with face fully made-up, whereas Lee and I are casually clad in shorts. I note that when Anita brings my Diet Coke, with a cloth napkin, no less, her nails are painted and manicured perfectly, and they look almost ethereal against the leaded glass that, to my delight, is one like my grandmother used to have, with etched ridges along the sides.

Everything in Lee and Anita's house seems to have an elegant comfort to it, and I find it easy to settle in, enjoy the pleasure of an iced Coke on a Sunday afternoon like so many I enjoyed at my grandmother's so long ago. I feel at home at their place and with them, and as they begin to tell me their stories, the child joins us, riding in with her legs wrapped around Lee's waist. I immediately hear the precise diction and neutral accent of a Midwestern voice coming from their little girl, and this is such a surprise, because both Lee and Anita have deep, rich Southern syllables that roll leisurely as this slow Sunday afternoon. I ask if the child has been raised at daycare at some point by somebody who was not Southern, but Lee and Anita shake their heads.

Later, when little Mary has left the room, we discuss that that Mary's speech must somehow be "the donor coming out."

Anita and Lee have never met Mary's donor, but they know a lot about him. They carefully picked out who he would be from files at a California sperm bank. Lee describes that, in her usual manner of carefully considering every important decision, Anita was so fastidious in researching the integrity and cleanliness of the place that would supply their child's seed that Anita insisted they travel over 1,400 miles to visit the sperm bank.

"I wanted to make sure the floors were clean, that everything was clean, and I wanted to see for myselfthat those men were tested and that the files were really there," Anita laughs. "And we spread those files all over the clean floor and looked at every one of them before we could decide."

"And I want you to know that our biggest fight came right there on the floor of that place!" Lee says. "Anita wanted this guy who was all creative-like, and I told her, 'No, you're artsy-fartsy enough—that'll come from you. If we've got to decide, we're going for brains!'"

"And I was insulted by what she said," Anita remarks, laughing.

I have already been amazed at little Mary's maturity. I had mistaken her for a first-grader until they told me she had just turned five and would be entering kindergarten next year. I have watched her reading words and remembering long sentences as she played with a wooden block story-building game.

"But I was right about the brains," Lee adds, "though, of course, Anita is smart, too. I just thought intelligence in the donor was important."

"Well, of course, it is. But then we also started fighting about if we would allow the donor to find out about Mary and Mary to find out who he was when she was eighteen. I was all right about that."

"But I didn't want some guy coming in here eighteen years later and wanting something from her, or wanting to suddenly be her parent. It just seemed too big a risk," Lee said.

I remark about how much of their lives together have involved taking such public risks—that Anita and Lee were quite courageous to openly be a couple, then have a child, and to live in a neighborhood that had always seemed so conservative to me. And, to top it off, Anita, Lee, and Mary attend a fairly traditional church where same-sex couples are not the norm, and they send Mary to a prestigious day school in which most of the other parents are heterosexual couples, many of whom are members of the town's most powerful families.

"I always assume everything is going to be OK any time we take a new step, and it seems like it always turns out that way," Anita says, smiling the wide open grin, that I am sure made her well-liked and always approachable in her hometown, with a population just less than 8,000 in a rural part of a neighboring Southern state. "Now, I don't want to say we flaunt our sexuality or throw it in people's faces because we are not like that. We don't want to make it an issue; we just want to live our lives as best we know how for us and for our child. Before we joined our church or sent Mary to school, we sat down with people and interviewed them, told them we were a couple and were both Mary's mothers and asked them, flat out, if we'd be welcome. I think if you're direct with people, they'll be honest with you and respect that."

Both Anita and Lee seem to want to give Mary the kind of neighborliness and caring community that they both experienced as children in Southern rural communities.And it is painful, I can tell, when Anita and Lee talk about how their coming out resulted in Lee's having extremely limited contact with her family—in fact, the family is cold toward Anita, and did not acknowledge Anita recently when Anita sat at Lee's bedside for three days after a recent surgery.

Anita reports that only one of her childhood friends approached her when she attended church in her hometown, but that she was touched by her friend's gesture.

"She said, 'Are you happy, honey?' and when I told her, 'Yes', she hugged me and said, 'Well, then, I'm happy, too.'"

Anita was raised in the conservative Church of Christ, in which members do not usually dance or drink alcohol, and church hymns are sung with no musical accompaniment because members believe the Bible does not direct the playing of musical instruments during worship services. Anita reports that most of her childhood and college friends, to this day, refuse to answer her letters or calls, and they think Anita's being committed to and preferring a female partner, "is a choice."

Lee and Anita both laugh when they tell me that prior to college, neither one of them had ever considered any other life than that of the typical American nuclear family in which they themselves were brought up.

"We both planned to finish college, marry a guy, and have children," Lee said. "It never occurred to me that I would be married to a woman."

When I asked how they had thought they were going to survive being married to a man if they were really attracted to women, Lee and Anita explained that they were so used to growing up with the traditional structure of their families of origin that they just figured that was really the only way to live—that no alternatives were really possible, if they wanted to raise children, without being completely rejected by society as they knew it. Their moves to the city changed that.

I remark that it seems so ironic (and even, amusing) to me that they have constructed a very conservative-appearing family life, in the ultimate WASPY neighborhood, and that they, in some ways, resemble the classic 1950s family tableau—attending church (in which they are very active); Mother baking and shuttling Mary from one wholesome activity to the next—t-ball, church picnics, birthday parties. Except, instead of the pensive dad smoking a pipe, Mary has two adoring moms.

Anita tells me a story about one of Mary's friends (the daughter of a heterosexual couple) who would always go to her father and ask for things because, "Mary has this or that." And the father would say, "Yes, we can do that," and would always dutifully go purchase the desired item.

"Until one day, " Anita says, "the little girl goes home and tells her father, 'Mary has two moms!' and her father says, 'Now, Honey, I damn sure can't do that!'"

We laugh and laugh, and then Lee gets kind of serious and says to Anita, "Tell her about the best compliment we ever got—at least, I consider it a compliment."

"I do, too," Anita agrees. "After we got to know some of our friends really well, the couple, a man and a woman, told us that when they're with us, they forget that we are two moms and that they are a mom and a dad—they just think of us as what we are, a family—a family that they care about and are proud for their child to know."

And then it hits me: they have truly achieved their own unique version of the American dream. Just as my great-grandfather, the son of a German Jewish immigrant, built this neighborhood as part of his American dream, Anita and Lee now live here, raise their child, openly present as a committed couple, and have become a loving family. Theirs is a quiet, personal movement, ignited by the need to live out their dream as fully and as honestly as they can. Their dream would be more fully realized if they had the same privileges as heterosexual couples do—Lee would be able to share legal custody of Mary; they could have health insurance for the entire family, instead of Lee's having to pay an additional $900 per month to buy a private policy to cover

Mary and for Anita to have additional maternity benefits that will cover the second pregnancy they hope will occur soon.

But, for now, as their child runs happily from one mom to the other, in this comfortable home on a beautiful street, they are grateful for what they have, and they credit God for making it possible. God, for them, is infinite love who has divine reason for everything, including leading them to find and love each other.Some people in their community would regard this belief as an abomination, but Anita and Lee know that their lives are no such thing. Just one look into their child's eyes is enough to remind them that divine love can be personified, can be represented in more sacred unions than some people in this society will ever be fortunate to know.

"We are blessed," Anita says. "We are so blessed."

Indeed, they are.

Gay in Malden, Massachusetts

John Gilgun

I was born in Malden, Massachusetts on October 1, 1935. The artist Frank Stella was born there on May 12, 1936. Both Frank and myself were almost certainly born in the same maternity ward in the same hospital. It's possible I might have met Frank Stella had he gone to Malden High School as I did. But his father sent him to Phillips Academy in Andover, Massachusetts, from which Frank moved on to Princeton.

Frank's parents were professional people and first generation Sicilian-Americans. His father was a gynecologist. My people are Irish-American and though my father's family had moved into the middle class (they owned their own milk company), my father was the black sheep of the family and broke with his family to work for Hood's Milk, delivering milk from door to door for thirty years before he was fired because of his alcoholism. My father was taken out of Catholic school in the eighth grade and put to work delivering milk for the family business at seven dollars a week. My mother left school after the eighth grade to work in a five- and ten-cent store. She worked all her married life as a waitress. As my mother used to tell me, "You were born to get up every morning and go to work. What else yuh got goin' for yuh?"

The difference between Frank Stella and myself is a difference of ethnic identity and socio-economic class. But what's Malden about if it's not ethnic identity and socio-economic class? I'm gay. Stella is straight. You're gay in Malden, eat my knuckle sandwich. What else is Malden about?

My earliest memories are of aggression. We lived in what's called a three-decker, three flats stacked on top of one another with airy back porches and a flat, tar-paper roof. The building was owned by a man named Bertocci. His son, Junior, who was a year older than me, beat me up daily until my mother told my father that we had to move. I was always told that the reason we moved is that I couldn't and wouldn't defend myself against Junior. But is this the real reason? Last month I wrote to my mother's sister, now 89 and living in a retirement home, and she replied, "All I remember about that house is that it was a terrible place and too cold in winter." But the story I got was, "We moved because you wouldn't fight back."

We rented a flat in a two-story house across from a city park. I had no interest in softball, which boys played in the park from March until mid-October. They played it compulsively, maniacally, as if their lives depended on it—and it probably did. They played no other games. I threw like a girl and couldn't hit the ball or catch it. I encountered the same aggression in the city park that had led to us to leave the three-decker. By the age of four I must have decided, "Who needs this shit? Why not play with girls?"

Girls played more interesting games than softball, including "house," where I dressed in my mother's clothes and played the mother. Since our house was across the street from the park, everything I did was done in full view of my peers fanatically playing softball there. It sealed my fate if my fate needed any additional sealing. I was "that sissy kid who plays with girls and dresses like a girl."

The park was surrounded by a chain-link fence eight feet high. Sometimes the softball made it over the fence, and I'd be on the street. Someone would yell, "Hey, kid! Get the ball. Throw it back in here." Because I threw like a girl, I could never get that ball over the fence. I had to shove it under the fence. The shame I felt at never being able to get that ball over the fence has never left me. To avoid the fence and the subsequent humiliation, I'd walk a mile out of my way to get home from school. Anything but that fence and... "Hey, kid! Throw it back in here. OK, you can't get it over the fence. Shove it under the fence then. Ha!"

I was forced by my mother ro play with the boys there. She'd watch from a window after she shoved me out of the house and toward the park. I'd always be chosen last—"We don't want him! Why don't you take him?—and humiliated while up at bat—"Easy out! Move into the infield!" To this day I hate baseball with every bone in my body, with every blood cell, with every breath that moves through my lungs. My mother loved baseball. My mother was butch.

"Why are you such a panty-waist?" She would scream. "Get outta the house into the park and play!" But it was a game I could never win.

From the first grade until the fourth I had only one friend, Norman, who must have been a gay kid, also. We played with puppets and we ran away from the tough kids who tried to beat us up. Finally, my mother broke up my friendship with Norman and set me up with a "real boy" named Hugh. Hugh and myself met only once for an hour. During that hour, we tossed a softball back and forth without saying anything, mindlessly, automatically, silently. It was like working on an assembly line for an hour—and perhaps that's what the game of catch prepared working-class boys for. If we were lucky, we'd get a job some day on an assembly line and bring home good money. We'd function like robots for eight hours a day every day of our adult lives, brainlessly, numbly, blankly. Then, after work, we could get drunk. We could hang out at Mullaney's. Then we could stagger home to beat up the old lady and traumatize our kids. That's what real men did.

After an hour of this torture with Hugh, I said I didn't want to do this anymore so Hugh shrugged and picked up his ball, and went home. Since my mother had broken off my friendship with Norman, I had no friends. How did I spend my childhood? I read a lot. "Get your nose out of that book! What's wrong with you anyhow?" Real boys don't read books. Nor do they get good grades. Nor do they write.

At the age of seven, I was reading on a fourth grade level. Though only in the second grade, I told my mother, "I want to be a writer when I grow up. Tell me the difference between 'too' and 'two.'" She used to take the books away from me and shove me out onto the street where real boys were laying wait for me. If I ran, I was a panty-waist. If I stood my ground, I was hamburger.

There was a branch library on the corner of our street. I read all the children's books there and begged for a dime so that I could take the city bus to the library downtown. I had a childhood of ticking clocks, the smell of floor wax, signs reading SILENCE and the comforting smell of library paste. I was safe in the library. Of course, I had to be shamed for hanging out there. Real boys don't.

Finally, to make a real boy out of me, my mother talked my father into renting a camp—actually a shack on the edge of the woods—for the summer at Martin's Pond in North Reading, Massachusetts. I was supposed to make myself into a real boy there, and I did.

The boys there did not play softball. It was if they never heard of the game. Maybe they couldn't afford a ball. They were all post-Depression poor. They had no park. They had the pond instead. With them, I learned to swim, to row a boat, to shoot with a bow and arrow, to fish, to catch turtles, and to play "war." I even had a slingshot. I went barefoot. I was Tom Sawyer.

A woman who worked with my mother as a waitress came to visit us that summer and said, "I heard you've become a real boy up here." Yeah. If Pinocchio can do it, so can I. I even learned ju-jitsu by reading about it in a comic book, and I managed to get one of the other boys on the ground and sit on top of him. I told him I would let him up if he said "uncle," and he said it. He was a skinny kid nicknamed Brother who had nine older sisters and never got enough to eat. He was so weak a sparrow could have knocked him over. But I did it and got a real boy point on my chart for doing it. I'd arrived. I was real. I beat up Brother. Oh wow.

Interestingly enough, North Reading was only a mile from Andover, where Dr. Stella would enroll his son Frank five years after we rented the camp. I think I may have seen the grounds with its trees and walks and white buildings with neo-classical columns at that time, though I didn't know what it was. In my mind now, I see all that smug Yankee upper-class glitter as a golden door opening onto a polite, civilized world where boys do not automatically knock you down, spit in your face, and call you a homo.

I imagine myself now with a secret benefactor like Pip in *Great Expectations.* Suddenly, I have the money to enroll at Andover. I kick the industrial dust of blue-collar Malden off my Converse sneakers, burn my jeans and t-shirts and raggedy Fruit of the Loom underpants and buy a wardrobe at J. Press. Like Frank Stella, I get chinos and Bass Weejuns and blue button-down shirts. Hey, Stella! Let's go back in time and start over. I've got money now and I can enroll at Andover. Room with me in the dorm on the quad. Sit beside me in chapel. Teach me to play lacrosse.

When I played with girls at the age of five, we played an the doctor-and-nurse sexual games a kid can play at that age, and I was hot for girls. After being shamed for playing with girls, I told them I couldn't play with them any more, then I had sex with Norman. I mean, we played, "You show me yours and I'll show you mine." After my mother broke up that friendship and I re-invented myself at Martin's Pond, I never had any interest in girls sexually. When I discovered I could masturbate to the point of orgasm at the early age of eleven, I never had a single image in my mind of anyone who was not a boy like myself. At the age of seven, I was in love with *Batman*'s Robin in his green lizard-skin shorts. I was obsessed with the bulge in Captain Marvel's crotch in its red union suit. Shazam!

I can't tell you I was born gay since I was hot for girls until the third grade. So, I have to believe that if I had not been shamed for playing with girls, I'd have grown up straight, a kind of effeminate-acting straight man who fucked women like my father. "You're just like your father!" my mother would yell. She was right. Genes rule. My father was a sissy, too, but he fucked women and drank himself to death in an attempt to hide his lack of manliness. No wonder he hated me. I was his worst nightmare realized. I was—himself.

How lucky I was to have woken up gay at the age of eleven. Wasn't I a boy? Didn't I have a boy's dick and couldn't I do things with it? And couldn't I do things with other boys' dicks? By the age of twelve, every boy was doing something sexual with other boys, and I fit right in. This lasted until I was fourteen, and then, since I rejected girls at the moment I was suddenly supposed to like them again, I "had a complex," and I was back at Square One. "What's wrong with you, anyhow? You don't like girls?" Duh.

At the age of fifteen, I gave up on Malden. After my sophomore year in high school, I told my parents I wasn't going to spend the summer sitting on the front porch, staring across the street at that bitch of a city park. I was leaving to go to work in New Hampshire. I had to come back from that job in September to sit blankly through my junior year in Malden High School. But, the following summer, I took a job in Maine. I had to come back to sit, depressed and wishing I was dead, through my senior year in Malden High School. But then I spent the summer after my graduation at the same job in Maine. Everywhere but in Malden I was considered perfectly normal. In Malden, however, I was persona non grata.

Persona non grata! What the fuck is that? Talk English, for Cristsake. Whaddaya mean, mental? Whadda yuh, some kind of fuckin' fruitcake? Jesus Christ almighty, what's wrong with you anyhow?

Meanwhile, in another universe called Andover that couldn't be less like Malden though only twenty miles up the road, Frank Stella was discovering art. Malden High School offered no art classes. And I learned nothing there.

Malden High School offered no such oasis. I learned nothing there except how to sit in the back of a classroom, scowling and counting the days until I could be released. It was a prison, and I recognized it as a prison. I was being confined there until I could be sent to work or war. After all, as a working-class kid, that's what I'd been born for—alienated labor and war. As one teacher said to another when she didn't think I was listening, "What are these boys except cannon fodder?" Graduation and then Pork Chop Hill in Korea. But I was already hearing stories about how fairies were weeded out at the induction center. So, where did that leave me?

Across the street from the high school was the city library, housed in a magnificent Richardson Romanesque building. I educated myself there since I was not being educated at Malden High School. By my junior year I was reading Dickens, Orwell, Salinger, F. Scott Fitzgerald, Hemingway, Faulkner, Norman Mailer, Thomas Wolfe, James Joyce, Robert Frost, John Keats, Wilfred Owen, and Shakespeare. Of course, if

I checked out a book of poetry, I kept it hidden under my sweater in public because only queers read poetry.

I was working at dead-end after-school jobs, so I had money. To get out of the meaningless classes I was forced to sit through, I paid a fee to take a series of aptitude tests administered by Boston University. You took the tests in the high school auditorium and you got out of classes while doing it. I had already won three National Scholastic Awards with writing I'd submitted to the regional (New England) National Scholastic contest. But winning something for a piece of writing was fag stuff, and I was humiliated for winning those awards. My picture was in the paper, and my mother's brother saw it and said, "You look like a fuckin' Jew!"

"John has a flair for writing," an English teacher told a class I was in after I'd won those awards. The derisive laughter rattled the chalk in the chalk tray. I wanted to crawl under my seat and die there while staring up through the slats of at Eugene Millhauser's seat at his divine ass.

The results of the Boston University aptitude tests were sent back from the university to a guidance counselor named Miss Crow. My rating for linguistic aptitude was so far off the charts that Miss Crow phoned my father and said, "Your son should go to college. He has the ability to do well there." My father answered, "What's a college?"

Boston University gave me additional tests in Boston at the university itself and I kept scoring on the genius level in linguistic aptitude. So the university accepted me into the freshman class at their school of Public Relations and Communications. I would be a journalism major because there'd be a job working on a newspaper for me when I graduated. I could ride subways into Boston. I could live at home. My father wouldn't have to pay room and board. Tuition was only a few hundred dollars a semester and both my parents were working. They had the money. No sweat for them.

My father said, "Well, what good is he anyway? I can't see him taking a job. Guys don't like him. He hasn't got a friend in the world. So, why not? Let him go to school. He's a hopeless case."

So I was on my way out of Malden, not through Andover which led to Princeton, but through BU which, led, after four years, to the Iowa Writers Workshop at Iowa State University in Iowa City.

Iowa! People smiled at me in Iowa and called me "John." People didn't roll their eyes and ask what was wrong with me because I read books. In Iowa City, everybody read books. No one laughed at them for reading, and no one said they were weird because they wrote stories and poems. All the guys in Iowa City claimed to be writers. For the first time in my life, I was in the majority.

I hear Malden's still there, sweating under its tattle tale gray, blue-collar sky. I've heard that gay guys live there openly now. They buy three-deckers and gentrify the neighborhood. They drive around in their Hondas and feel no fear. Hey, I'll take it on faith. I'm not going back to check it out. Va-va-vroom. I'm outta there. I ain't goin' back.

Growing Up Gay in Dixie

Louie Crew

This essay was written in 1976-1977

I am a male, 40, openly and happily married to another male. We make our home in rural central Georgia, where he is a hairdresser and I am an associate professor at a state college. I am white; he is black. We are active in the community and have valuable friends on the campus and in town, where we have lived for almost four years.

Growing into my present open, reasonably stable, maximally fulfilling gay consciousness has been a circuitous, tedious process, with many false starts. My background was similar to that of many native Southerners. Great-great-great-granddaddy was a private in the South Carolina troops in the Revolutionary War. Great-granddaddy fought as a private in the Coosa County, Alabama, troops of the War of the Rebellion. I was born and reared in Anniston, Alabama; went to prep school at McCallie in Chattanooga; went off to Baylor University in Texas with a view to becoming a Baptist preacher; and wound up a schoolteacher, first at Auburn University, then at Darlington prep school in Rome, Georgia, and later at the University of Alabama, where I earned my doctorate in English.

My world of Anniston, Chattanooga, Tuscaloosa, Atlanta, and Auburn did not give me much help in growing up as a gay person. The thousands of gays in the South who had come before me were never allowed any positive visibility, and my entire education was directed by people who were not gay and who were unable to understand me.

The only gays I heard about in my youth were victims of cruel gossip, most typically people unlucky enough to have been caught in their own efforts to conceal themselves. They were always roundly vilified. Almost every small Southern town I know about has its tale of some talented person who was forced to leave following the "scandal" of such discovery. Most often the "crime" at worst was having been involved in an act of nonviolent affection of mutual consent, or often merely having made the inquiry to someone to discover whether he or she would be interested in such a relationship.

Growing Up Alone

My boyhood in the South was Puritanical, heavily influenced by the church. During puberty, I learned about masturbation from two fellows who had discovered it at a Boy Scout camp. I realized as we did it together that they had a fascination for me that resembled their own fantasies about girls they were going to try this with. About the same time, my Baptist preachers talked in vague, compelling terms about "secret sin." For evidence of the preacher's truth I carried in my wallet a group picture of my masturbation buddies, a seventh grade snapshot made in the buff when about five of us had had an overnight party at my house. I remember my grandmother's initial surprise when she once discovered the picture. "What's this, son!?" she said. And then her face grew as inscrutable as the sphinx, as if stolidly certain of what I was vaguely beginning to know for myself. My attraction to these fellows was at once a compelling mystery and my shameful secret.

At puberty, I struggled to be faithful to my church's condemnation of homosexual behavior by denying my sexuality altogether, except for frantic autoeroticism and its attendant same-sex fantasies, which kept my secret ever before me. Had I been straight, the dynamics would have been the same but the institutions of courtships, dating, the family, etc., would have counterbalanced the internalized guilt over masturbation. As it was, so effective was the restraint which I accepted, that by the time I was twenty-eight, I could count on eight fingers my personal experience of orgasm with other persons.

At prep school once, some friends were discussing wet dreams. They shared some of their fantasies, and asked me to do so. When I told how in one of my wet dreams a kind old man sitting next to me on a bus had reached out to touch me, one of those amateur psychologists with a great show of concern gave the accurate diagnosis: "You must be becoming a homosexual yourself." I knew he was right, but I was scared beyond imagining at his discovery. I wished that I had not shared the dream; I wanted to recall it, annul it, but I knew that the dream corresponded with everything my body had always told me about myself. The effect of my friend's discovery was to reinforce my commitment to sexual self-denial. Thereafter I chose far more carefully those to whom I spoke about my "thorn in the flesh. "

I buried myself in work and won the award for "unselfish service." And I often spent long hours staring off Chattanooga's Missionary Ridge, wondering about a previous winner of the award who had committed suicide, so the student rumors went, because he feared exposure for homosexuality. When a student—one I thought least like the stereotype that we circulated—was summarily sent home for having required a younger student to perform fellatio on him, the events warned me of the risks of ever acting out my own sexuality. I minimized all personal contact except the most institutionalized, and had my touch only by serving as the campus athletic trainer, torturing myself with the unreciprocal physical rubbings of all my heroes. Growing up gay in a military school was a formidable challenge.

Fortunately, I did not retreat altogether from close contact with people during the years after boarding school. Instead I worked hard at developing five very close and long-term friendships with other males, most of them college classmates or colleagues. We shared comprehensive intellectual interests as well as a common professed disinterest in sexual behavior of any sort. To each of these select few I "confessed" my homosexual inclinations, but always in such a way as to seek the individual's support of me in my resistance to such "temptations." I studiously avoided any person I suspected was homosexual, naively assuming that I was an expert at such recognition. I could not accept the truth that just as I do not fit homosexual stereotypes, so are most other homosexuals equally unrecognizable. I made it expressly clear to my friends that I did not want reciprocal sexual confidences from them, and most complied. Year after year, we traveled thousands of miles to visit and wrote scores of letters. It was not until I was 28 and beginning at last to face squarely my own needs for human genital contact that I began to see that most of my bachelor "intellectual" friends were also homosexual and most were also committed to a fierce celibacy.

Except for the limited sharing of these early "confessions," being gay for me meant being terribly alone, always having to wear a mask, constantly justifying even to myself my lack of sexuality by saying that I thereby won some spiritual compensations. Freud's word *sublimation* came along as a big help: At least I knew better than to repress, and as much as I hated myself for doing so, I spent myself tirelessly in autoeroticism and prayer.

Sublimation was grim, but it did have some rewards. I certainly grew as a student. Often I also was able to be a good friend. Ironically, I was to respond better to the needs of others than to my own. As a corridor master at Darlington, I was trusted to keep a secret and frequently was asked by a distraught student: "Sir, what am I to do?! I have just blown my roommate!" Here I was, never having known a gay adult whom I trusted and never having had the courage to act out my own attractions, yet called upon to counsel others.

"Did you enjoy it?" I asked.

"Yes, that's what scares me," always was the reply.

"Did he enjoy it?" I asked.

"I don't know."

"Well, aren't you talking to the wrong person?"

I am still amazed at my good sense as I recall those sessions in which I had to play it by ear, instinctively leading persons away from the very guilt that was suffocating me. Somehow I always knew that the crucial question was the personal one: "Have you looked for a way for this experience to bring you closer to another human being?" It seemed terribly important to tell them what I knew then mainly from books, but know now in the flesh: They were not isolated freaks for having had such sexual experience and their enjoyment of the experience did not commit them irrevocably to repeat such behavior.

Not the First

I was in my thirties before I learned that a major religious figure in my childhood daily cruised the local bus station for homosexual trade. When, once at college, I went for counsel about my incessant homosexual dreams, the preacher opened the door and asked his secretary to stay within earshot, so fearful was he of being closeted with someone even to discuss gay dreams. Four years later, this same preacher was fired for having an affair with his male choir director. When, as a teenager, I once shared with a fellow convert at a Billy Graham rally what I had written as my confession in the booklets that were handed out for this purpose, the gorgeous young man confessed in tears that he too was "guilty," and then in fear we both avoided each other thereafter. At Baylor, I once slipped an anonymous note under the office door of my religion professor begging him to discuss homosexuality in our Christian ethics class; instead, he gave a grim lecture on the Freudian terms *id*, *ego*, *superego*, and suggested that his "anonymous caller" (I turned crimson!) ought to see a psychiatrist, and a Christian psychiatrist at that.

In short, I was facing in the South what gays face everywhere: I could not become visible without becoming an outcast; older gays were unwilling to risk counseling the young; nongays did not understand the experience at all and were often openly hostile.

When I started teaching at Auburn, I discovered at the Opelika bus station my first glory hole, an orifice in the wall dividing toilet stalls that accommodates anonymous sexuality. Later, I discovered that those holes abound on most Southern campuses, particularly in libraries and in union buildings. At Auburn, I was amazed to discover some of the brightest professors and students making their rounds to cruise the johns. At the University of Alabama, I learned that gay sex was big business, particularly in certain key departments. At least one dean and three department heads were well known to our gay underground. Yet this underground offered very little community or support, and only on the rarest of occasions the dubious privilege of a nude swimming party or a one-sex dance. And even on those occasions, people were fairly uncommunicative, and most did not even participate, so great were the risks of any potential visibility.

Amazingly, many gays survive these conditions and manage to avoid being crippled by society's fears, and our own as well. Many of us manage to preserve our integrity and to make meaningful contributions at all levels of society. Strangely, only in 1973 did the American Psychiatric Association "discover" what many gays have known all along: Our gayness is not the sickness; the sickness is the homophobia plaguing the land.

Our society finds it especially difficult to grasp the fact that we gays can repress or "control" our instincts without ever changing—much less "curing"—our gayness. I myself was once pressured by a psychologist to accept heterosexuality. I found myself capable of heterosexual responses, responded to the overtures of a young woman with whom I could be completely open about my predominantly gay orientation, married her, and had a successful sexual relationship, as measured by the actual pleasure given and received. Yet throughout our five years together, I sacrificed my primary orientation, my sense of self, my wholeness, my integrity. Now I am amazed that our society would license people to practice such counsel, that our society would encourage in young women a missionary zeal to "convert" men, that parents would rejoice at such suspicious "salvation," and that a priest would rejoice in such a marriage, knowing all the facts, but would not rejoice to see two men who love each other undertake the same union. If we have a messed-up, confused, alienated, crumbling society, as I suspect we do, I believe that we have ourselves to blame. For starters at reform, we might try an honest avowal of our own nature and desires, instead of merely conforming to a code of institutionalized behavior thrust upon us.

Coming Out

Our culture teaches that homosexuality is the perversion of heterosexuality, and for years I believed it. Only slowly did I realize that the real perversion is the deceit and duplicity with which too many persons, gay and not gay, continue to live.

In my many years in the closet, I found Southern writers sometimes managed to break the silence and speak about people who shared my sexual orientation, but often the accounts were more devastating than the silence. Calder Willingham in *End as a Man*, writing of his experiences at The Citadel, speaks of a brutality that completely violates my gay sensibilities. Tennessee Williams peoples his works with self-destructive gay neurotics, thus earning for himself the title "Poet of the Damned." The gay male in Truman Capote's *Other Voices, Other Rooms* is an ominous, mysterious threat, and the novel's little boy is routinely teased by freaks and circus people. Southern gothic novels spread damnation-by-association like sorghum over the gay experience, a heavy sweetness unto death that is not likely to tempt any reasonable gay person to walk out of safe hiding. Even hints of camp, of gay celebration, when they occurred in Southern fiction, were usually played for their jadedness. The impression I received was that all gay sexual encounters were grim and joyless, and that grand old families were routinely leveled by them. Neither impression has been confirmed by my own experience of healthy, open gay sexuality.

For years, I took it as a blessing that I was not very effeminate, was not usually recognized as gay, even in the highly sensitive boarding schools where I taught, where sometimes even straights were fired for giving the misleading impressions of feminine softness. Of course, I studiously avoided any clues of gayness, real or imaginary. I would never wear green on Thursdays, always kept my fingernails closely trimmed, eschewed various "delicate" styles of smoking cigarettes, and crossed my legs about as assiduously as I avoided football and rough competition. I now have no particular regrets about the sexual blend that resulted in my personality. And I even enjoy my renaissance notion of mixing a certain toughness with a definite gentleness. What I do resent is that my culture made me pay the heavy price of sexual abstinence for twenty-eight years to maintain this view of myself.

In the closet, I was unlikely to find a strong gay love relationship that could nourish my wholeness. In the closet, I could not affirm my casual existence as a gay person on a par with my sexual existence. In the closet I maintained the rigid, stultifying separation of my mind and my body. In the closet, I was even afraid to pray to my God, "Just As I Am," and no church thought to tell me that the God who made me loves creation and designed my body chemistry. I had left the Baptist church to become an Episcopalian at age twenty-five and, though the form of worship was more pleasing, the needs of my body and personality to be reconciled were still not met. In the closet I wasted holy energy of all sorts—intellectual, spiritual, artistic, sexual—trying to be something that I was not, namely a heterosexual.

My real growing up was accomplished in 1973 when I decided to leave the closet. I announced to my classes and to the community that I was gay. I accepted, affirmed, and celebrated being who I am. Two major factors influenced this dramatic reversal of my habits of thirty-seven years. For the first time I was involved in a gay relationship in which both of us desired a long-term, substantial commitment, and we were both much too happy in our own union to be willing to hide. In fact, we felt that many public dimensions of healthy unions (shared colleagues, friends, economic relationships, etc.) required such openness if we were going to have a space for growth. Secondly, I had been given an opportunity to co-edit *College English* for a special issue on "The Homosexual Imagination" (Vol. 36, No. 3, November, 1974). In doing so I wanted to speak my pronouns honestly, not they, them, their and theirs, but we, us, our and ours.

When I announced my gay identity, the world did not fall apart as I had feared; in fact, for the first time it really began to make sense. By embracing myself, I discovered, even actualized, my strength, my energy, my capacity to love, my ability to be loved, my will to survive as myself rather than as a fabrication of my community. For the first time, many major ideas of our culture began to make sense in terms of my personal experience, not the least of which were Grace, Redemption, The Wandering Jew, The Good Samaritan, Integrity, etc.

In the closet, a gay inevitably confirms the might of the oppressor, and the social and economic mobility allowed to those who pass as not gay is bought at the price of self-doubt that the oppressor is right. As Dr. King used to say, "Those who go to the back of the bus probably deserve the back of the bus." To think oneself a slave is the worst form of slavery; it is to be shackled with what William Blake called "mind-forged manacles." Homosexuality is a serious felony in 34 states, but the real measure of the oppression is in terms of the quiet resignation of the thousands of gays who do not complain. My vulnerability is measured by the tight closet doors of many about me.

Gay mind-forged manacles rattle across our land, growing rusty, ready to break. Thousands of gays wait to make their own discoveries of growth into personal freedom and responsibility. I have met gay people of every race, class and background working in every area of the South. It is high time for the South to grow up to the needs of these gay persons. At this time, gays remain the one minority group with no outspoken allies, in spite of the fact that all gays are born in heterosexual unions. Few if any sympathetic non-gays are self-confident enough in their own sexual orientation to risk being seen wearing one of our buttons. Politicians are terrified of open association with us, though they frequently knock at the back door and are regular, if anonymous, customers at gay baths. Schools which we support with our taxes maintain medieval notions about us and systematically deprive us of our history while flagrantly appropriating as non-gay most of the literature, music, and art that we have created. Medical servants and public health officials are not even trained to understand basic specialized requirements of gay patients and typically give us inadequate physical examinations. Religious groups, for the most part, regularly condemn us as special sinners, and social groups ostracize all of us who refuse to be invisible.

The most immediate and specific need of gays is the extension to us of our civil rights. We should have the freedom of sexual association and public overtures of affection as do non-gays. We should not be discriminated against in employment, housing, etc. Our marriages should be accorded legal status, and possibly even tax credits should be awarded us for our contribution to solving both the population explosion and the energy crisis. Television, movies, and textbooks should be required to give a full view of the gay experience from uncensored gay points of view. Every care should be made to recognize the diversity of ways of life in the gay experience, not just those styles which confirm non-gays' fears of us. Crimes against gays by blackmailers, entrapment specialists, toughs and other hooligans should be punished with firmness. Children should be guaranteed an atmosphere of freedom and joy in which to discover more responsibly who they are and who they may become.

If this vision of equality is too terrifying to America and the South, perhaps we should rewrite the tenets of our church and state institutions more honestly, saying instead that "whosoever is straight and believeth in Him should not perish but have everlasting life," and that "all straights are created equal and endowed with certain inalienable rights."

The Declaration would be narrower, the Gospel less good news, but such revisions would do justice to those straights who are afraid they might be gay if given a fair chance to discover who they are.

Growing up gay in the South is a challenge, one that became exciting for me only when I assumed responsibility for my own growth. During my nearly thirty-seven years of acquiescing to the bleak invisibility prescribed for gays, I abetted the arrest of my own healthy maturation.

Now I routinely face a different set of problems, namely, the hostility which our society reserves for open gays; yet I face this hostility with maturity and with the energy I formerly wasted in hiding and self-hatred. It has been painful to be cut off from some members of my family, though fortunately my parents have remained supportive, though confused. Some of my neighbors' children spit on me when I jog and shout obscenities as I routinely pass through town. HUD has proved that a local real estate agent discriminated against the two of us by denying housing when he learned that we are gay and racially integrated. Because I am gay, a dean in another university refused to hire me, though I was the unanimous choice of the entire search committee and of his thirty-member faculty rank and tenure committee.

Several members of the vestry at my local parish sent a letter asking me to "find some other place of worship that may be more in sympathy to your thinking and efforts toward gay people," and when I shared this letter with the press, my bishop blew up and told me through the papers that he was summoning me for discipline, because I (!) had "disturbed the peace and good order of the Church." [See *The Peace of Christ is Not for Gays*] Interestingly, at the "discipline" session he admitted privately to my lawyer and to me that he had "no authority to discipline a lay person" and had spoken only in anger, but he has refused to make this episcopal abuse clear to the public.

Another bishop (in the Anglican Orthodox Church) wrote a letter printed on the front page of the regional Birchite paper accusing my lover and me of having caused the tornado that ripped through our town recently! Meanwhile, my priest sometimes shouts at me in public, has said that he wants to kill me, and sometimes spills the communion wine on me when I continue to accept Christ's invitation for all persons to partake of His body and blood. Confronting such nonsense from the changing old order is much easier than was the task of trying to accept that order's definitions of me.

In the mutual support and understanding of our union, my spouse and I daily confirm all that our culture had taught us about gayness was indeed a denial of our full humanity. It is a real comment on the quality our society gives to gay life that the two of us met just outside the bathroom on the sixth floor of the Atlanta YMCA. Such a fact might be a source of shame in the straight culture, but is a source of pride and joy in the gay culture, evidence of the staying power and growing power of the gay experience—no matter what kind of ground the straight culture allows us to plant in.

My growth is not the decadence of my family tree, but the flowering of the dreams of freedom that my great-granddaddies had in the American Revolution and the War of the Rebellion. My gay integrity, wholeness, honesty, and responsibility are part of an honorable human tradition, and the New South will simply have to make room for Ernest and me.

Two Grooms

Fort Valley, Georgia, 1976

Our marriage, on February 2, 1974, like our courtship, has been conventional. It was love at first sight when we met at the elevator just outside the sixth-floor bathroom of the Atlanta YMCA on September 2, 1973. Ernest was a fashion coordinator for a local department store; I was a state college professor from 100 miles way, deep in the peach and pecan orchards. One of us black, the other white, both native Southerners. We commuted every weekend for five months. Our friends were not surprised when we decided to marry.

We would have wasted our time to send an announcement to the local papers. Besides, the bank employees spread the word just as effectively when we took out a joint account. Our wedding itself was private, just the two of us and the Holy Spirit. Parents, although loving, would not have welcomed the occasion; our priest would not have officiated even had he been granted the Episcopal authority which was expressly denied. Two apartment neighbors, historians, sent a bottle of champagne; a psychologist friend dropped in earlier to propose a toast; others sent welcoming tokens.

We unloaded the heavier gear from the car before beginning the ceremony. Then we carried each other across the threshold into the dining room, where the table was set with two wine glasses from Woolworth's, one lone and lighted red candle instead of our customary two green ones, a vase with one early narcissus, and an open *Book of Common Prayer.* We read the service nervously, its fearsome bidding and pledges. The words "woman" and "wife" translated readily as "spouse," "man," "husband," person. It all took only about ten minutes.

One could be too quick to sentimentalize a few details, such as our bed, a two-hundred-year-old four-poster built by the slave ancestors of one of us for the free ancestors of the other. Perhaps we were fulfilling their dream? Or Dr. King's dream? We find day-to-day living too difficult for us to negotiate other people's dreams. We work at living our own dream, a dream no different from the dream of many other couples, a dream of a home with much love to bridge our separateness.

After the Honeymoon

Our careers have always been very important to both of us. We came together from the beginning anticipating many of the inevitable tensions between our rival commitments to careers and to each other. We both had already enjoyed professional success in a variety of occupations; our main challenge was clearly going to be whether or not we could succeed together. One of my biggest hesitations during our months of courtship was my fear that I might thereby seem to commit myself to conjugal activity as much of the time when we lived all of our time together. Little did I realize that Ernest too enjoys working alone many days on end for fourteen to sixteen hours a day.

Ironically, earlier lessons from our oppression as relatively less conspicuous gays served as resources for our thriving as an openly gay couple employed behind the Cotton Curtain. Gays learn very early that most jobs are not secure for those even suspected of being gay. Very early on, Ernest had been fired from a civil service job when he refused to go to bed with a male supervisor, who then had Ernest "investigated" and "proved" gay. All of my teaching assignments have been filled with horrifying anecdotes about various predecessors who were fired when discovered as "queer." The effect of this clear pattern of discrimination was the same on both of us: Prepare for as many jobs as you possibly can; never go into real debt; own mainly portable property; be able always to land on your feet.

Before we met, Ernest had supported himself with a variety of jobs—janitorial service, modeling, fashion coordinating, nursing. I had worked as a lumberjack, mechanic, professor, professional actor, waiter, writer. We both know that when push comes to shove we can always be caterers, seamsters, peach pickers. What is more, we know that we would be better than most at any of these tasks. We have simply had to be sure of this kind of mobility. Tenure is always meaningless when one is gay. I have never expected an institution to grant me tenure, and I have always been an excellent teacher precisely because I am willing to take the kinds of risks that are necessary to germinate ideas, the very kinds of risks that disqualify one with tenure committees.

This is not to deny the anxiety that accompanies threats to any job security, and certainly not to support those threats, but merely to put those threats into a perspective where we have been able to negotiate them reasonably successfully with, more important than any one job, our integrity preserved. Humor has been a saving factor repeatedly. When Ernest went to apply for beauty school, for example, the white ladies who ran the place were terrified at the idea of having a black male there, assuming that his only motive would be sexual assault. When he sensed their fear, he explained to them that he was married to another man, and they took him in with open arms.

Imagine the response that came after a bishop from the Anglican Orthodox Church wrote to the local paper saying that the two of us, by organizing a national group of gay Episcopalians, had been responsible for the devastating tornado that recently struck Fort Valley. That tornado left the two of us and our property unharmed but knocked the steeple off every homophobic church in the white community. "Would one expect God to keep silent when homosexuals are tolerated?" the bishop asked. That evening, in a spate of hate calls, one familiar voice rang: "Louie, you and Ernest get yourselves on over here and kiss in my backyard so my greens will grow!" An administrator at the college also called to suggest that I apply for head of Agriculture: Power to control the wind and the rain is queer power indeed.

Professional paranoia is an occupational necessity for open gays. Right now I have in litigation a complaint against a major American university [pun intended] where I was denied employment by a homophobic dean after my winning the unanimous support not only of a search committee of faculty and students but also of the entire thirty-six members of the college's faculty rank and tenure committee. Damaging evidence is still being sent to me by the members of that Committee, who are irate that the dean violated due process and hired a candidate who had received absolutely no support. More typically, job applications for advertised positions never receive answers at all.

We have been no freer from domestic harassment. In August 1975, after a year of investigation, HUD found our complaint true that a local real estate agent had discriminated against us in housing because he considered us to be criminals. Still HUD had no enforcement powers; the agent refused to conciliate; and no lawyer would take the case for contingency fees, knowing, as one lawyer said, "the predictable response of the juries in this part of the country."

Meanwhile, in the white lower-middle class neighborhood where we live, nightly as I jog I am spat upon and verbally reviled by the eight-, ten-, and twelve-year-old children on bicycles, as their parents sit on their porches relishing vain hopes that their children will not grow up to be queer. Night after night, as Ernest has returned from cosmetology classes, he has feasted on their verbal ingenuity, purposely taking up to ten minutes just to get his kit out of the car. There would be no help in protest. The police would only arrest us for "child molestation" or "contributing to the delinquency of a minor." The local Baptist preacher has already sent us a copy of a letter which he sent to the sheriff urging investigation.

For a long time, our friends here wondered why we do not at least keep a lower profile by not mentioning our relationship. It is important to Ernest and me that our relationship is public. We are not in merely a sexual union, but in a complex coupling that integrates all our life together. Whether we are entertaining or being entertained, even when we are just shopping at the local Piggly Wiggly, it is important for us to know that we know that they know. We can even sometimes get into enjoying their games with knowing, as when the employees all dash behind the butchers' one-way mirror to watch us wink at them when we pass. As Ernest puts it, "Honey, you may gloat, but we're the stars!"

White men have been having sex with black men in the South since 1619, yet such homosexuality has always been related negatively to straight institutions and defined as adultery, fornication, or sodomy. Our open marriage obviates these definitions. The effect is sometimes to move friends and neighbors into a new state of consciousness. Rarely, if ever before on my almost all-black campus, has a man proudly and publicly sported his white male spouse; rarely, if ever before, has a white man in Georgia proudly notified his family, prep school, even his chapter of the Sons of the American Revolution, of his happy marriage to a black man. If the profile is memorable, far more important is the seriousness we ourselves have experienced in this bonding.

Some of our friends elsewhere have accused us of masochism, saying that we ought to leave as soon as we get employment that is as challenging and fulfilling as that we now have, but no place is clearly enough a haven for gay persons to justify our leaving at a cut in pay or taking jobs that we would not find fulfilling. It may very well be an indictment of the so-called liberal white American universities that they leave to a small, struggling, rural black college the admittedly difficult tasks of adjusting to an outspoken gay scholar. Interestingly, the same people who accuse us of masochism frequently control or at least influence jobs to which we might flee. At times, it is difficult to stifle the bitter awareness of the eloquence with which they would write of our being lynched.

Our economic resources have been diverse, including Ernest's earnings from nursing and then from various student employments while studying cosmetology—including his unemployment checks for which he qualifies only because the state refuses to recognize our marriage, and including my salary as an associate professor, which remains conspicuously below that of unpublished but non-gay colleagues of the same rank, as revealed in the Georgia state auditor's annual report. Speculations are legion as to why I have not been fired. I prefer to think that it is because I am lucky enough to have a chairperson who knows that I am a good teacher. She feels that none of my life, public or private, is of any concern to her unless it relates directly and immediately to my function on my job. Bosses higher up are more mixed. One official called me in almost immediately after my serving notice to students and officials that I am gay; he said that he respected my courage. So did the chairpersons of at least two other departments. One very prissy boss, however, is threatened and brings visitors periodically to tut outside my office. When Ernest similarly refused to do the work of an orderly while having the rank of an LPN, the hospital employer called him "uppity." When he tried to organize the black aides to demand rights being denied them, they balked in fear and the hospital fired him.

One of the lowest points in our marriage was an occasion when I asked Ernest, "If you get that job with the cosmetics firm in NYC, can I live off your earnings so I won't have to stay here in Georgia the rest of this year?" He did not answer. I waited out the long silence almost half a day, and then he said, "Did I ask you could I 'live off your earnings' when I moved here from Atlanta without a job first?" I had momentarily lapsed from the more pervasive economy that our marriage effects. Were we autonomous, at each trysting we would come at each other unequally. I would be the wealthier, Ernest the younger; I the more experienced, Ernest the more spontaneous. In marriage everything is given once and for all. For us, marriage ended trading and introduced sharing. The money is ours. The youth is ours. The spontaneity is ours. And whatever is exhausted or whatever is incremented is ours.

We find the marriage changes in kind the range of our personal and material security. Expressed negatively, Ernest gave up his fashion training in Atlanta to become a low-paid LPN in a rural hospital; I gave up a Fulbright to Turkey, where he would have no chances of employment. Ernest gave up his LPN so that we could be together for my summer as an National Endowment for the Humanities fellow at Berkeley. I took on our full support for several months while he was in school. But the negative way of viewing our material existence ignores what we gained. By such choices (we do not even call them sacrifices), we have effected the very possibility of working together. Both careers give and take from a union that is richer than either career or than any of our possible independencies. At least we perceive ourselves richer, and as Flip Wilson's drag character Geraldine says, "What you see is what you get!"

Although we are not likely to be altogether free of them ourselves, we find that many heterosexist ways of merely asking questions about relationships create problems for the relationships. "Who makes the money?" "Who spends the money?" "Who owns the car?" "Who owns the fur coat?" "Who owns the motorcycle?" "Who pays the rent?" "Who does the dirty work?" "We do!" is our answer to all these questions.

My own neurotic compulsions with these middle class perceptions have frequently inhibited my full enjoyment of our marriage. While I enjoy cooking, sewing, and more limitedly, keeping house, more and more my writing and my organizing activities have preempted the major portions of my energy. Ernest is a better cook, a much more efficient housekeeper, and an expert shopper. Once, I came home late on a rainy night to find all the washed wet clothes in the refrigerator. "What on earth!" I exclaimed.

"Lord, chile, you sure be white tonight," he laughed. "I can tell your mama never took in washing. It's the way to avert the mildew."

My learning to enjoy my man's househusbandliness as much as I enjoy my own is in many ways parallel to our enjoying all parts of each other's anatomy. The first question most gay friends ask us is, "Which of you is the husband? Which the wife?" We honestly have no way to answer respecting this dichotomy. We are not thus differentiated. We both like gentle perfumes, and we both like poignant funkiness; we both enjoy our gracefulness as well as our toughness.

We are not mirror images, however. Our careers are different and we do not compete. We make no special demands about productivity, but we are both aware that a marriage is dead when either fails to want to contribute. Ernest respects the summers I spend not making a dime but writing away as if I'll not have another such season. I respect his taking off a year to go to school or his taking time off to do hair of women in the state mental hospital.

We also easily resist unhealthy veneration of each other. He is wisely suspicious of much of the pomposity of the academic community, and I of much of the vanity of the cosmetic industry. Each of us is mature enough in his own career not to need much reinforcement, at times even to require deflation. I doubt that the two of us could thrive very long together if we did not know that we definitely can "make it" apart. We are committed to a relationship precisely because it is "unnecessary." Of course, in a temporal sphere that we choose to cohabit we do need each other and we are able to be vulnerable, but we are careful never to require a longer rope than can pull each back to his own boat and anchorage. We are not drowning men clawing at a lifeguard, as seems to be the model fashionable in much nongay media these days.

At the risk of being still more invidious, I suspect that many nongay couples up because society's alleged support of heterosexual relationships is falsely advertised and hypocritical. After the honeymoon is over, once the careers pull at each other, once Jan and John realize that their parents might even expect them to divorce, that their priest has divorced, that their friends and neighbors are too busy with their own relationships to care (except possibly for the value of self-congratulation that attends efforts to seem to care), non-gays choose to walk away from each other in bewilderment, or to remain together only by law. Gay relationships may be paradoxically blessed by not having the chance even to expect such support systems.

Ernest and I wrote our divorce contract at the outset: Each would take half. We made our wills to structure property guarantees. We both own together all that each makes. We have had to make our own structures, knowing that major efforts would be exerted to deny even those plans. We have instructions about funerals, burials, etc.

We have had some few but very significant resources in our community, namely, in our friends. We are both gregarious and affable, and we are invited to many parties. Often he is the only black person or I the only white person present, so segregated are the others in our community. We are avid dancers, and always do courtesies of dancing with our hosts' spouses. Maybe some index of our integration is the fact that only one couple has ever said that we should feel comfortable to dance together at their parties, and even there the other guests do not have an ambience about them that would make us feel comfortable doing so. Also, our gay friends would be much too vulnerable for us to invite to gay parties any of our nongay friends.

In many ways, we did not even anticipate that our coupling is itself our career, so much does it alter our professional expectations, our job security, our work climate, etc. Everyone knows that gay folks are reasonably harmless if we remain at the baths, the bars, the adult movie houses, the tearooms, and other such restricted areas. Ernest could have met a new Louie and I a new Ernest every night at the Atlanta YMCA for decades, and no one would have bothered much. Possibly a Tennessee Williams might have celebrated our waste, or maybe even a Proust. Certainly my priest would not have shouted, as he did recently, that we are "making a mockery of Christian marriage and the home." Then my bishop would never have written, as he did this week, "I am weary of almost constant pressure applied on this office by a movement which I do not fully understand, but which I wish to grow in understanding"—this while virtually telling me, probably his only regular gay correspondent, that I persecute him merely by calling attention to my needs and the needs of my people. Were Ernest and I still just tricking furtively at the YMCA, my students would see me as they used to, as the linguist, the rhetorician, the literary critic, the poet, the jogger—and not, as so often now, merely as "that smart sissy." It is only when we couple openly that the heterosexist culture marshals its forces against us.

The bonding we share has made us take greater risks in thought and action. As open gays actively fighting a very hostile environment precisely because of our sexual orientation, we have at home the quiet strong security of our love always attesting to the rightness of our public claims and countering the wrong attitudes about us that even we might otherwise find hard to resist. It has been impossible for us to doubt the beauty and the holiness of gay love in general when morning, noon, and night we have known the beauty of our gay love in particular. In the past, I somewhat tentatively fought from the closet for gay rights for others to be happier than I ever had been or expected ever to be; today, I would fight openly to the end just for the two of us to be as happy as we are. Paradoxically, with "community" thus strongly narrowed to just the two of us, I simultaneously feel much more fully a part of the struggle of all gay sisters and brothers everywhere and for all times.

Contributors' Notes

DAVID-MATTHEW BARNES ("The Lady of the House") is known for and committed to creating powerful literary material for women and minorities. He is the writer and director of the film *Frozen Stars*, and the author of the popular novel *Ambrosia*, three poetry collections and twenty-five stage plays. His short stories, poetry, and creative non-fictional works have appeared in over fifty magazines, literary journals, and anthologies, including *The Best Stage Scenes of 1999*, *The Best Stage Scenes of 2000*, and *The Best Gay Love Stories 2005*. A two-time Elly Award winner, his stage plays have received over two hundred performances across the nation and internationally in South Africa, Brazil, Taiwan, England, and Western Australia. Two of his plays, *And The Winner Is…* and the ever-popular *Are You All Right In There?*, are published by Playscripts. In 2004, *Somebody's Baby*, *Temporary Heroes* and the teen-fave *Unrequited* were published by Brooklyn Publishers. Some of David-Matthew's most critically-acclaimed stage plays are available in print from Lulu Books: *Darling Among The Maidens*, *False Hopes*, *Frozen Stars*, *Number 76*, *Pensacola*, *Sloe Gin Fizz* and *Thenody*. He and his partner, award-winning producer Nick Moreno, live just outside Atlanta. You can see more of David-Matthew's work at www.davidmatthewbarnes.com.

DARIN BEASLEY ("Start With A Farm") studied under the tutelage of Tom Spanbauer in his Dangerous Writing program. During that time, Beasley wrote and completed his first novel, *Slaughter Me*. He is at work on short nonfiction and a series of connected short stories. He has lived on the West Coast since 1990 and presently resides in Portland, Oregon. He can be reached at darinevanb@yahoo.com.

ANGELIQUE CHAMBERS ("Sweet Home") received her bachelor's degree from State University of New York Oswego. She lives in upstate New York with the two loves of her life: her partner, Sarah, and cat, Kitty. Her poems appear in the 2004 summer issue of *Bloom*. This is her first nonfiction publication.

LOUIE CREW ("Growing up Gay in Dixie" & "Two Grooms") is a Professor Emeritus at Rutgers, The State University of New Jersey. He is the author of over 1,500 publications. He holds a PhD degree from the University of Alabama and honorary doctorates from three Episcopal seminaries. He serves on the Executive Council (Board of Directors) of the Episcopal Church USA. He and his spouse, Ernest, are members of Grace Church in Newark, NJ.

NANCY DEMPSEY ("Their American Dream") is a freelance writer with numerous publications. She travels the U.S. in search of great stories.

JOHN GILGUN ("Gay in Malden, Massachusetts") is the author of *Everything That Has Been Shall Be Again*

(Bieler Press, 1981); *Music I Never Dreamed Of* (Amethyst Press, 1989); *From the Inside Out* (Three Phrase, 1991); *The Dooley Poems* (Robin Price, 1991); *Your Buddy Misses You* (Three Phrase, 1995) and *In the Zone: The Moby Dick Poems of John Gilgun* (Pecan Grove Press, 2002).

CHARLES JENSEN ("New Kid In Town") lives in Tempe, Arizona, where he teaches at Arizona State University and works for Hayden's Ferry Review. His poetry has appeared in *Colorado Review, Brooklyn Review, Portland Review, 42 Opus,* and *Folio.*

CURT JOHNSON (Foreword)is a producer and writer. He earned his first producing credit before graduating college with *Common Threads: Stories from the Quilt* which won the 1989 Academy Award. After college, he became a London correspondent for *Rolling Stone* and *Spin* along with producing music videos for emerging artists such as Suede, East 17 and M People.

Returning to America in 1995, Curt moved to New York City where he began his public relations company, New World, Inc. while writing for television shows such as *The X-Files, Titus, Once and Again*, and *Roswell* among others.

After successfully promoting other people's projects, Curt decided to combine his two passions, producing and writing, and created his own production company. His first project, *Thoth* won the 2002 Academy Award. *West Memphis Three* is the second production through his company, and he will also serve as Executive Producer on the title soundtrack with

Kid Rock; along with writing the movie/book tie-in for Bantam Books.

Curt's upcoming projects include *Walk On*, feature film with director Walter Hill; along with *The Duke*, biopic about heavyweight champ Tommy Morrison, whose career ended when he tested HIV-positive in 1996; and *Priority One*, an original television series.

TRACI LYNN ("The Long Ride Home") a Screen Actors Guild Joseph C. Riley Award recipient, is an actress, voice-over artist, and a screenwriter who has performed extensively on the New York and London stages. She has had numerous television roles, including guest appearances on *Law & Order, Criminal Intent* and *All My Children*, as well as appearances on *The Sopranos* and *One Life to Live*. Traci was honored to perform Sara Scopp's *Lady* for PBS, which was also very well-received on the London stage. Traci shares a beautiful life with her partner, dividing their time between New York City and lovely East Hampton.

JAMIE NELSON ("Listen") is originally from Livingston, NJ, but spent most of her life in Florida. You may recognize her as one of the *Sesame Street* kids from the 1970s. Jamie spent many years traveling with a carnival, while studying her schoolbooks along the way. She is an award-winning clarinetist, competition dancer, and yoga fanatic, and she holds degrees in psychology and communication from The Florida State University. Jamie has hosted live radio shows from Tallahassee to Tucson to Miami, and currently New York. She has been the voice of Clairol Herbal Essences,

Starbucks, Advil, *The Montel Williams Show*, The Discovery Networks, and literally thousands of commercials, radio, and TV stations. Jamie has been a reporter, emcee, dancer, broadcast consultant, motivational speaker, and owns a voice-over and broadcasting school in Manhattan. In her free time, you can see Jamie doing nothing, because she has no free time, and she likes it that way.

HAWK MADRONE ("Shikse Tomboy") has been living on remote women's land in southern Oregon for almost thirty years, where she purposes to do Tai Chi as a way of life. With her animal companions always nearby, she is a woodworker, gardener, photographer, baker, teacher, and writer. Madrone's poetry and poems have been published in *Womanspirit, Common Lives/Lesbian Lives, We'Moon: Gaia Rhythms for Women,* and *Maize*; and in the anthologies *Our Lives: Lesbian Personal Writings* (Frances Rooney, editor); *The Poetry of Sex* (Tee Corinne, editor); *The Wild Good* (Beatrix Gates, editor); and *An Intricate Weave* (Marlene Fuller, editor). Her memoir, *Weeding at Dawn: A Lesbian Country Life*, was published by The Harrington Park/Haworth Press in 2000.

JEFF MANN ("Loving Mountains, Loving Men") grew up in Covington, VA, and Hinton, WV, and received degrees in English and forestry from West Virginia University. His fiction, poetry, and essays have appeared in many publications, including *The Spoon River Review*, *Wild Sweet Notes: Fifty Years of West Virginia Poetry 1950-1999*, *Prairie Schooner*, *Journal of Appalachian Studies*, *Laurel Review*, *The*

James White Review, The Gay and Lesbian Review Worldwide, Rebel Yell, Crab Orchard Review, West Branch, and *Appalachian Heritage.* He has published three award-winning chapbooks: *Bliss* (Brickhouse Books, 1998), *Mountain Fireflies* (Poetic Matrix Press, 2000) *Flint Shards From Sussex* (Gival Press, 2000). Appearing in 2003 were a collection of essays, *Edge* (Haworth Press) and a novella *Devoured,* included in *Masters of Midnight* (Kensington Books). Another collection of poetry, *On the Tongue,* will be published by Gival Press in 2006. At present, Jeff lives in Charleston, WV, and Blacksburg, VA, where he teaches Appalachian Studies, creative writing, and literature at Virginia Tech.

ELIZABETH NEWMAN (Editor) is a therapist who specializes in counseling at-risk and traumatized children. She practices in rural Arkansas. Prior to completing a Master of Science degree in social work, Beth earned an MFA in creative writing at the Iowa Writers' Workshop, The University of Iowa. In her spare time, she is a publicist for a rock singer and rescues Newfoundland and St. Bernard dogs.

KENNETH POBO ("Ovaltine Dreams: Growing Up Gay In Villa Park, Illinois") has just released a book of poems *Introductions* (Pearl's Book'em Press). His poems, essays, and stories have appeared in *Queen's Quarterly, Mid-America Review, Rattle, Timber Creek Review, Nimrod, Philadelphia Inquirer Magazine, Heaven Bone, Hawaii Review, Colorado Review,* The *Fiddlehead*, and *Apalachee Quarterly.*

PETER ROGNLI ("Roller Skates") is an unemployed graduate of Bemidji State University's creative writing program. He currently resides in a tent in the forests of Northern Minnesota where he spends his summers working as a Boy Scout camp counselor—two months of the year when he is definitely not gay. Editor's Note: This author's note was composed by Pete himself!

STACEY WAITE ("About Ben")is a visiting lecturer in English-Writing at the University of Pittsburgh. Originally from Long Island, Stacey was the winner of the 2004 Frank O'Hara Prize for Poetry for her collection, *Choke*. Her manuscript, "Butch Geography," has been a finalist in over 15 national competitions, including the 2002 National Poetry Series and the 2003 Paris Review Prize for Poetry. Her work has appeared most recently in *The Marlboro Review*, *West Branch*, *5 AM*, and *Nimrod*.

CHARITY WARREN ("My Familiar") is a native Texan, a freelance writer, and an artist who has found a new home in the Pacific Northwest. Her spare time is split between teaching martial arts, cycling, and loving life with her partner and two cats.

ESTHER WILLISON ("A Womanly Thing") is one of the founders and teachers of an alternative public school in Schenectady, NY, 1970-1985. Most recently, Esther was the assistant director of a teen theater project that brings AIDS education into the public schools. Her work has appeared in *The Stories We Hold Secret*, *Common Lives/Lesbian Lives*,

13th Moon, *Harrington Lesbian Fiction Quarterly*, and *The Litchfield Review*. She has just completed a memoir about her daughter, Andrea. Esther is currently on staff at The Open Door Bookstore in Schenectady, NY, has a daughter, Judith, and a partner, Barbara, of 23 years.

ALAN WITCHEY ("Waking Up In Fifth Grade") was born and raised in Indiana, but now lives in Irvine, CA, with his partner of fifteen years and his dog Wicca. He will earn his MFA in Creative Writing from Antioch University in December 2005.

Printed in the United States
21779LVS00001B/55

9 780966 074499